HISTORICAL SKETCH

OF

OLD HANOVER CHURCH,

BY

REV. THOMAS H. ROBINSON, D. D.

WITH A NOTICE

OF THE

CHURCH AT CONEWAGO,

BY

A. BOYD HAMILTON.

PUBLISHED BY THE
DAUPHIN COUNTY HISTORICAL SOCIETY,
1878.

Notice

In many older books, foxing (or discoloration) occurs and, in some instances, print lightens with wear and age. Reprinted books, such as this, often duplicate these flaws, notwithstanding efforts to reduce or eliminate them. The pages of this reprint have been digitally enhanced and, where possible, the flaws eliminated in order to provide clarity of content and a pleasant reading experience.

Originally published
Harrisburg, Pennsylvania
1878

Reprinted by:

Janaway Publishing, Inc.
2412 Nicklaus Dr.
Santa Maria, California 93455
(805) 925-1038
www.janawaygenealogy.com

2010

ISBN 10: 1596410159
ISBN 13: 9781596410152

Made in the United States of America

PREFATORY.

THE Publication Committee of the Historical Society of Dauphin County, in pursuance of one of the objects of its organization, to preserve the records of the early settlements of the county, take pleasure in presenting to its members the second number of its contributions to the historical literature of this locality—the proceedings and addresses on the occasion of the Centenary of Independence, July 4, 1876, being the initial publication. The present pamphlet comprises

1. HISTORICAL SKETCH OF OLD HANOVER CHURCH. By Rev. Thomas H. Robinson, D. D.

2. NOTES RELATING TO THE CHURCH AT CONEWAGO, AND THE NEW-SIDE GRAVE-YARD IN LOWER PAXTANG TOWNSHIP. By A. Boyd Hamilton.

The history of Old Hanover Church will prove of great value, especially for its genealogical data, meagre though that may be, and will be highly appreciated not alone by the members of the Society, but by the descendants of the many good and true whose dust lies within the stone-walled enclosure on Bow creek, a tributary of the Swatara, three miles from Manada Gap. The record given in these pages comprises all information accessible worthy of preservation. The Notes relating to a Congregation of Scotch-Irish Presbyterians of which little has been known, will also be an acceptable contribution. In the hope that these records herewith presented will awaken more anxious inquiries and tend to the preservation of every letter, document and newspaper relating to the biography or early history of our county of Dauphin, the Committee submit with pleasure the following pages.

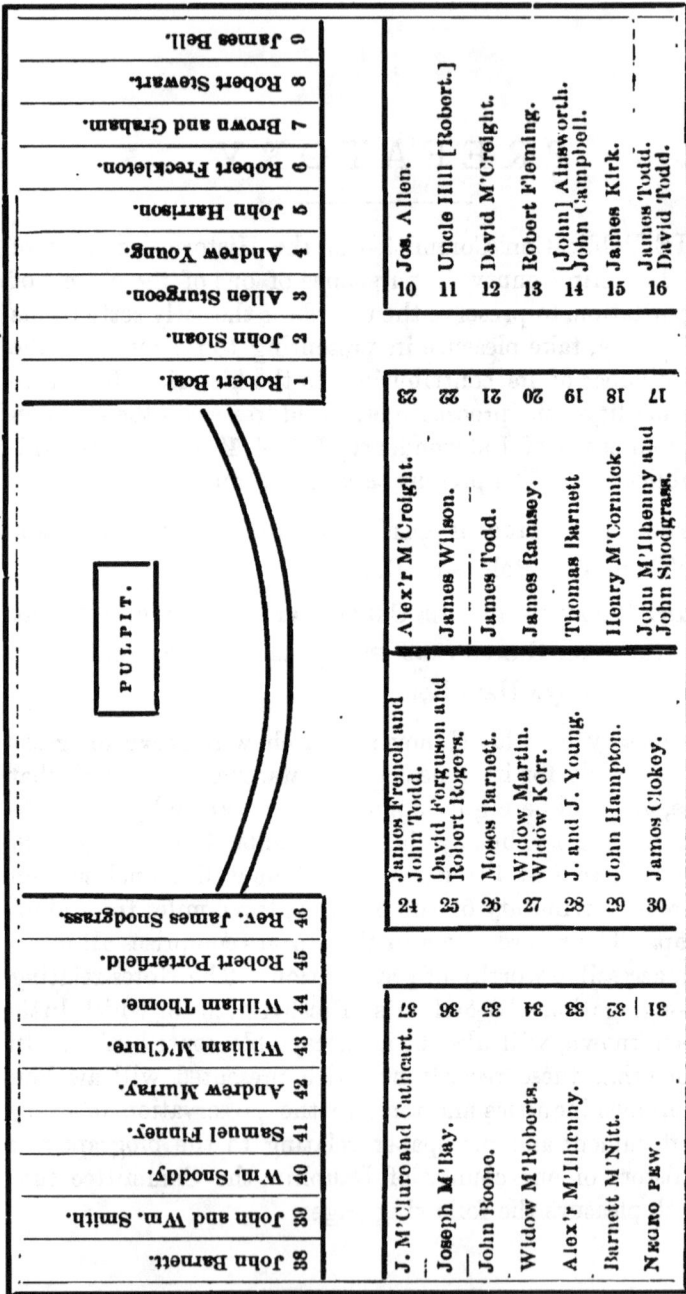

PLAN OF HANOVER CHURCH.
(Occupants of Pews about 1800.)

EARLY HISTORY

OF

OLD HANOVER CHURCH,

DAUPHIN COUNTY, PENNSYLVANIA.

By Rev. THOMAS H. ROBINSON, D. D.

INSCRIPTION ON THE INNER FRONT WALL OF HANOVER CHURCH.

[The following inscription was cut on a large stone formerly occupying a place in the front wall of the Church, high up. This stone, since the demolition of the Church, has been lying in the grave-yard, and the lettering, owing to its exposure, can only be discerned by the fingers :]

HOC TEMPLUM,
REV. ADMODUM JACOBO SNODGRASSO,
CONCORPORATO PRO CŒTU HANOVERENSI
A JOHANNE M'FANDIENE ÆDIFICATUM
A. D. 1788.

INSCRIPTIONS IN HANOVER GRAVE-YARD.

In Memory of
The Rev'd MAT. WOODS
who died Sept'r 13th 1784
in the 27th Year of his Age
and 3d of his ministry.
During the short term of his ministry
he approved himself as a diligent
faithful Servant of CHRIST.
In him were united Learning, Judgment,
and eminent Piety, with great meekness,
self diffidence and humility.

This marble was the donation of
his affectionate People.

Serve *Christ* humbly on earth, if you
expect to reign triumphantly with
him in heaven.

Rev. JAMES SNODGRASS
Pastor of the Presbyterian Congregation
of West Hanover during a period of 58 years,
and 2 months. He was born in Bucks co. Pa.,
July 23d 1763
Licensed to preach the Gospel by the Presbytery
of Philadelphia in Dec. 1785. Ordained &
Installed by the Presbytery of Carlisle in
May 1788; and departed this life July 2d
1846, In the 84th Year of his age.

Your fathers where are they, and the
prophets do they live forever
Zech. I; v.

DEDICATORY.

THE following fragments of history, gathered from the minutes of the Presbyteries of Donegal and of Carlisle; the records of the Board of Trustees of Hanover Church, some very incomplete records of the last pastor of the church, from tax lists, tradition, &c., are respectfully dedicated to the descendants of "Old Hanover," by one of their number who has felt a special interest in rescuing from oblivion whatever memorials he could obtain of a church whose earthly history is ended, save as she lives in her widely scattered children. It has been deemed wisest in a few instances to preserve the ancient spelling of proper means. The

OLD HANOVER CHURCH.

original name of Old Hanover Church was Monnoday or Manada, the Indian name of a creek which, breaking through a gap in the Kittatinny mountains, becomes, after a few miles, a tributary of the Swatara. The old church stood about three miles from the mountains and eleven from Harrisburg. Visiting the place a few months ago, the writer found only scattered remnants of the ancient stone structure, and close by the walled grave-yard where the "Fathers of ye olden time" are sleeping. A fund for the repairing of the grave-yard, obtained by the sale of the church building and from other sources, is in the hands of a body of trustees. The building was in dilapidated condition and had been wholly unfit for the use of worship for a score or more of years. It was, as the engraving of it shows, a plain, stone, barn-like structure, but well adapted, by the strength of its walls, for the worship of many generations. The home of the last pastor of the church stands but a few rods away, and by the very gate of the parsonage yard there breaks forth, full and strong, from the hill-side, one of the many springs of cool, clear, delightful water, with which this entire region abounds. Here the thirsty worshippers of several generations refreshed themselves at the intervals of religious service. Two or three of the old families are still represented in the homes of the region, but the well-filled grave-yard, where many an unmarked mound, many a well-worn, moss-covered stone, with the better-preserved memorial of later times, may be seen, shows how large a Presbyterian ancestry once occupied this region. It would be pleasant to the compiler of these memorials, to receive from any of the descendants of Old Hanover to whom they may come, such further facts and traditions of the early times as they may possess. He would also take this occasion to return his thanks to his fellow-members of " The Historical Society " for very valuable aid in exhuming and preparing parts of this record; especially to those unwearied delvers after the history of the early times in central Pennsylvania, Messrs. A. B. Hamilton and W. H. Egle, M. D.

T. H. R.

EARLY HISTORY OF "OLD HANOVER."

1735. In 1735 the Presbytery of Donegal, then the only Presbytery of the Presbyterian Church in America west of Philadelphia, was in session at Nottingham, Chester county, Pa., in the month of September. This Presbytery had been created by order of the Synod of Philadelphia in September, 1732. The original members of it were Rev. Messrs. James Anderson, Adam Boyd, William Bertram, John Thomson and Robert Orr. On the 3d of September, 1735, a supplication was presented from "A people on the borders of Suitara Congregation, desiring the countenance of Presbytery in building a new meeting house in order to have supplies;" which being read, the Rev. William Bertram, the pastor of the Swatara Congregation, reported that his people desired him to signify to the Presbytery that they desire them to defer granting said supplication until they be heard. The matter was deferred until the next meeting of Presbytery.

At a session of Presbytery held at the same place, October 7, 1735, the affair of the people of Manada Creek was again deferred.

"Mr. Richard Sankey, a theological student from Ireland, having produced his certificate at last meeting before the members of Presbytery, and been taken under its care, the Presbytery ordered that he endeavor to acquaint himself with the brethren before our next meeting, and also endeavor to prepare some preliminary *extempore* trials against our next meeting."

At a session of the Presbytery held at Middle Octorara, Lancaster county, November 20th, *Lazarus Stewart* appeared to prosecute a supplication of Manada Creek for a new erection.

Rev. Messrs. Craighead and Anderson, who had been appointed to consider the matter of dividing Rev. Mr. Bertram's congregation, reported that the Congregation of Derry desired to be separated from Paxton as a distinct congregation, and to have their bounds defined. The Presbytery desired to be better informed about the distances

2

and situation of the people before coming to a decision in these matters, and appointed Rev. James Anderson, and "any brother whom the standing committee of Presbytery may designate" to act with him, to "perambulate the bounds and borders of the congregation of Derry and the people of Manada some time next spring, said brethren to take particular notice of the meeting house of Manada, its distance from the meeting house of Derry." They are also empowered to fix the bounds of said people, and to determine concerning the meeting house of Manada.

Paxtang, Derry and Manada, afterwards known as *Hanover*, were at this time under the pastoral care of Rev. Mr. Bertram, making a very large and widely scattered congregation. The meeting houses were at Paxtang and Derry, but as new settlers came in, and new lands were taken up, the boundaries of the congregation enlarged, and new meeting houses were needed. The people of Manada were settled along Manada creek, towards the Kittatinny or Blue Hills eastward and northward. The district covered by Mr. Bertram's charge was from fifteen to twenty-five miles in length and breadth, reaching from the Conewago creek to the mountains, and embracing all the people east of the Susquehanna, beyond the western line of the Donegal congregation, Rev. Mr. Anderson's. It was by common consent a law of the times, that meeting houses should be about ten miles apart, so that the people might not be compelled to travel too far for Sabbath worship. The formation of new congregations was often a matter of difficulty and much dispute, as was also the location of new "meeting houses."

The region along Manada creek to the mountains was settled rapidly, and the people early began to feel the inconvenience of going so far as Derry to church, and moved for a new "erection or congregation." At that early day they were all Irish or Scotch-Irish, and were connected with the Presbyterian church. The boundaries of congregations and the location of meeting houses were determined by the Presbytery with considerable authority.

At the meeting of Presbytery, November, 1735, Mr. Sankey, or Sanckey, or Zanchy, as the name is variously given, was questioned by Presbytery on Divinity and Philosophy, and having satisfied the body with his answers, he was directed to write a sermon on Prov. III, 6: "In all thy ways acknowledge Him," &c., to be read before the Standing Committee at their first meeting, who, if they see cause, shall appoint him another subject for discourse as a piece of trial at the next meeting of Presbytery. On December 10, 1735,

Mr. Sankey delivered his discourse on Prov. III, 6. It was approved and he was directed to prepare another for Presbytery on Psalm XLIII, 3 : " O send out Thy light, &c."

1736. On May 25, 1736, the Presbytery met at Nottingham. Rev. James Anderson, Mr. Andrew Galbraith and Mr. William Maxwell, a ruling elder from Paxtang, were ordered to meet on Tuesday before the next meeting of Presbytery at Derry, to be held on the first Monday in September, in order to perambulate the " bounds " between the people of Derry and Manada.

On May 26th Mr. Sankey delivered a lecture on the XXIII Psalm, which was approved, and he was ordered to prepare an exegesis or critical exercise on "*An Christus qua Mediator, sit orderanda.*"

Mr. Anderson reported that the perambulation between Derry and Manada had been fulfilled, and gave in the statements of the committee in writing. Debates and pleadings were had between the parties at length. Afterwards the Presbytery retired into " The little House." [This was a small building near the Derry church, which was used as a study for the pastor, and also as a room for the church session and other purposes.] After consideration and debate, the Presbytery resolved to erect the people of Manada into a distinct congregation, and approved the place where they had begun to build as most suitable for a meeting house. Mr. Lazarus Stewart engaged to the Presbytery that all persons who belong to or shall join themselves to the new erection, who are in arrears to Mr. Bertram shall pay up. On the next day it was agreed by the people of Manada and Derry, and ordered by the Presbytery, " that the people on the borders of these two congregations, that is, between the meeting houses and beyond the creek of Suitara, shall on or before the first of November next, declare in an orderly way, *i. e.* before some elder or principal man in the congregation, which they make choice of, whether they will join the congregation of Derry or Manada, and after said first day of November none who dwell in bounds shall be at liberty to alter their choice but by the concurrence of both the congregations or order of the Presbytery."

September 2, Mr. Sankey delivered his discourse on Rom. II, 3, and his essay on "*An Christus*," &c., both of which were approved, and he was ordered to prepare a sermon on Rom. III, 31, and also to be prepared to defend his thesis against next meeting.

October 26, *Mr. Lazarus Stewart* reported at a meeting of Presbytery in " Dunagal " that nothing had been done in paying arrears to

Rev. Mr. Bertram, because no list of arrears had been rendered, but that they were ready to act when an account is rendered.

October 27, Mr. Sankey gave a popular sermon, and was further examined in Languages and Philosophy, acknowledging the Westminster Confession and Catechisms, and promising to conform to the Directory, and to give subjection to the Presbytery, and was licensed to preach the Gospel as a probationer.

November 10, it was ordered that Messrs. James Gelston and Richard Sankey supply Pequea and Manada by monthly turns alternately until the next meeting of Presbytery.

1737. April 6, in pursuance of a supplication from the people of Manada, Mr. Bertram was ordered to supply that people on the last Sabbath of April, and to convene the people on some day of the following week, in order to *moderate a call to Mr. Sankey*.

June 22, a supplication and a call to Mr. Sankey was presented to Presbytery by *John Cunningham* and *Robert Grier*, commissioners from the congregation of Hanover, (Manada,) by which said commissioners are empowered to promise towards Mr. Sankey's support among the people of Hanover as their orderly pastor, the annual payment of sixty pounds, *i. e.*, one-half in cloth and the other in particular commodities, as flax, hemp, linen yarn and cloth, together with several gratuities mentioned in said supplication. Said call was recommended to Mr. Sankey's consideration till the next meeting of Presbytery. He was appointed to supply Paxtang and Hanover alternately, and to open the next meeting of Presbytery with a sermon from Rom. VI, 21.

PASTORATE OF REV. RICHARD SANKEY.

August 31, Presbytery met at Middle Octorara. Mr. Sankey opened with a sermon from Rom. VI, 22, preaching from that verse by mistake. The discourse was approved as a part of trial, and he was ordered to prepare an exegetical discourse on the Resurrection of Christ as a "common head." He accepted the call from Hanover, and was appointed to supply the pulpit till the next meeting of Presbytery.

October 6, Mr. Sankey opened Presbytery with a sermon from Mark XVI, 9, which was accepted as a part of his trial. The people of Hanover asked that Mr. Sankey's ordination and installation be hastened. He was ordered to supply them until the next meeting of Presbytery.

Mr. Sankey at this time got himself into trouble. It came out that he had sent to a Mr. Hunter, of New Castle Presbytery, a sermon containing some very considerable errors in point of important doctrines of religion. Mr. Hunter used the sermon as one of his trial pieces before the Presbytery, and was in consequence set aside by Presbytery. It was then agreed by the Presbytery that Mr. Sankey should be appointed as correspondent to attend a meeting of the Presbytery of New Castle, and clear up the matter. He went thither, and on inquiry it was found that he had sent notes of a sermon to Mr. Hunter, and that said notes did contain such errors as were reported, but that Mr. Sankey had not only condemned and laid aside such erroneous notes from all use, but had sent a letter of contrition with said notes to Mr. Hunter, which did not come into his hands. The Presbytery, after much and serious consideration, concluded that, although upon a serious review of Mr. Sankey's conduct both before and after his being preacher, we cannot see any ground to suspect him of unsoundness of the faith, yet we condemn as a great and gross imprudence his writing and sending forth such notes, and thereby giving such occasion for stumbling both to ministers and people, and therefore judge that he ought to be severely rebuked by the moderator for the same, and strictly cautioned to act with more circumspection for the future, and to guard against all offensive conduct either in this or any other kind. Mr. Sankey, being called in, was accordingly rebuked, which he cheerfully submitted to. He was ordered to deliver an exposition of Psalm XV, and to prepare a Presbyterial exercise from Rom. VIII, 4, at the next meeting. [P. S. The two passages seem to have been given as a reproof to Mr. Sankey's unrighteousness.]

1738. April 6, Mr. Sankey opened Presbytery at Donegal with an exposition of the XV Psalm. The Presbyterial exercise was deferred until the next meeting, and he was ordered to preach a popular sermon from John I, 29.

At the meeting in June, he delivered both the exercise and the sermon, and they were both approved. The next meeting of Presbytery was appointed at Hanover, on the last Wednesday of August, when Mr. Sankey was to have his extempore trial, and if approved, to be ordained and installed on the next day, the last Thursday of August, 1738. Rev. Wm. Bertram was appointed to preside.

August 30, the Presbytery of Donegal met for the first time at Hanover. Present: Ministers—Thomas Craighead, Alexander Craighead, William Bertram, James Anderson, Adam Boyd, John Paul,

Samuel Black, John Thomson. *Ruling Elders*—Matthew Atchison, Daniel Henderson, James Carothers, John Christy and Hugh Scott. Mr. Sankey gave his extempore trial, which was approved, and all other parts of trial, and it was ordered that he be ordained to-morrow. Richard Sankey was ordained and received as a member of the Presbytery of Donegal, and was installed as the *first pastor* of the Hanover church.

1745. The next reference to Hanover in the minutes of Presbytery is in June, when it met again at Hanover. The pastoral relation between Mr. Sankey and Hanover church is declared to be in a satisfactory condition. The people are, however, in arrears of salary. It was customary whenever the Presbytery met at a particular church to make a thorough examination into the condition of affairs. They first called the pastor before them in private and questioned him about the elders and the people; then they called the elders and questioned them about the pastor and people; lastly, the representatives of the people were called and questioned, in private also, about the pastor and elders.

1745 to 1750. * The Presbytery of Donegal and the churches were now passing through a stormy period—the period of the Old and New Light controversy, raised in connection with the revivals of Whitefield and the Tennents. The state of religion became shamefully low. The feuds were bitter. The ministry, by their conduct, brought reproach upon religion, and sometimes upon good morals even. The vice of intemperance seems to have prevailed, and even the clergy indulged to excess. There was also a looseness of morals made painfully evident in the reports before Presbytery. The records give, however, little history of the churches. The Presbytery became divided, the original Presbytery of Donegal adhering to the Old Light party. The minutes are very brief and were very negligently kept for years. But little business was done. They close very abruptly in 1750. Mr. Sankey was still the pastor of Hanover, but we have no history of his work there or of the state of the church.

Nine years of the records of Donegal Presbytery now disappear, and with these all history of the Hanover church. Mr. Sankey continued in the pastoral care of the church.

1759. In 1759, June 5, the records of the Presbytery of Donegal are resumed. Mr. Sankey is still a member of Presbytery and resid-

---

* The members of Old Hanover Congregation as early as 1750, less than twenty years after its founding, may be gathered from the list of taxables in Rupp's History of Dauphin County, p. 206.

ing at Hanover. At this period, from 1756* to 1764, the entire region was greatly harrassed by Indian wars. The savages, spurred on by

Hanover Ass'is for the King's Use, 1759.

	£.	s.	d.		£.	s.	d.
Andrew, John	0	2	6	Huston, Robert	0	2	6
Allen, Willim	0	3	6	Hutchison, Joseph, sen'r	0	2	6
Andrew, John	0	2	0	Hutchison, Joseph, ju'r	0	2	0
Brown, Patrick	0	2	0	Hay, John	0	2	6
Beard, James	0	2	6	Hums, Robert	0	2	6
Bell, Robert	0	10	0	Heanes, Bartholemew	0	1	0
Brown, William	0	2	6	Hutchison, John	0	9	6
Barnet, William	0	3	0	Harper, Adam	0	9	6
Brown, Andrew	0	3	9	Hetrick, Petter	0	2	6
Brandon, William	0	2	6	Huff, Joseph	0	1	6
Brown, Daniel	0	2	6	Hooke, Rudey	0	1	6
Bell, Thomas	0	5	0	Henderson, John	0	2	0
Bell, Thomas	0	2	6	Hill, John	0	2	0
Barnet, Martha	0	2	6	Humes, Thomas	0	2	6
Brown, Samuel	0	2	6	Haloback, John	0	1	0
Brown, John	0	3	0	Innis, Brice	0	10	0
Brown, John	0	9	6	James, Willm	0	9	9
Brown, William	0	2	6	Kinzer, Sebosten	0	2	0
Britebel, Gorge	0	12	0	Litel, John, Docter	0	10	0
Besor, Barnet	0	2	6	Lard, William	0	2	0
Besor, Mathi	0	2	6	Lard, James	0	10	0
Besor, Jacob	0	1	6	Merten, Alexander	0	2	9
Brown, Robert	0	2	6	Merten, Robert	0	1	6
Breden, William	0	2	0	Mountgomrey, Robert	0	1	6
Diver, William	0	1	6	Montgomrey, John	0	9	6
Dixon, John	0	9	6	McFarlan, Walter	0	3	6
Dixon, James	0	3	0	McColech, Alexander	0	10	0
Dermond, Marey	0	1	6	McCormick, Henrey	0	2	6
Endsworth, Samuel	0	9	6	McCord, John	0	2	0
Cooper, Willim	0	2	6	McClochane, David	0	1	0
Clamer, Adem	0	2	6	McClochanochan, James	0	2	6
Clark, William	0	1	6	McCormick, John	0	2	0
Clark, Benjamin	0	4	6	McCraught, Anten	0	2	0
Clark, James	0	2	6	McCluar, William	0	2	0
Campbel, John	0	3	6	McCluar, Thomas	0	2	0
Conygahm, Marey	0	1	6	McCluar, John	0	2	0
Curay, Robart	0	10	0	McCluar, Elener	0	1	6
Conyngahm, Elisebath	0	3	9	McClintock, William	0	15	0
Crawford, John	0	9	6	McColem, Alexander	0	2	6
Crawford, John, jun'r	0	3	9	McColoch, John	0	2	6
Counts, Henrey	0	2	0	McClure, William	0	2	6
Fargison, William	0	5	0	McCluar, ffrances	0	3	6
French, Thomas	0	9	6	McCluar, James	0	2	0
Foster, John	0	7	6	McCluar, James	0	3	6
Fray, Ruddey	0	2	6	McQuier, Thimothey	0	5	0
Fox, John	0	9	6	McQuion, James	0	3	0
Finey, Thomas	0	2	6	McQuion, John	0	5	0
Finey, James	0	3	0	McElheney, William	0	3	0
Finey, James, jun'r	0	5	0	McNutt, Joseph	0	2	6
Finey, Thomas, jun'r	0	2	6	McMullen, Thomas	0	2	0
French, James	0	2	6	O'heney, David	0	2	0
Glispey, Gorge	0	2	6	Park, James	0	3	6
Getey, John	0	2	0	Prist, Thomas	0	2	6
Graims, William	0	5	0	Prist, Meray	0	2	6
Graims, William, jun'r	0	2	6	Porterfild, Robert	0	2	0
Gililand, John	0	1	6	Rogers, Gorge	0	3	9
Grinlie, James	0	2	0	Ripeth, Jams	0	1	6
Graims, John	0	2	0	Ripeth, Hugh	0	1	6
Glenn, Hugh	0	1	6	Ripeth, William	0	1	0

the French, who were at hostility with England, made many incursions into the country along the Susquehanna. Hanover congregation, lying next the mountains, was greatly exposed, and the people

	£.	s.	d.		£.	s.	d.
Robison, James	0	1	6	Wallace, Robt	0	7	6
Rosemberey, Esmos	0	1	6	Wallace, Benjamin	1	0	0
Robinson, Effey	0	9	0	Willson, Joseph	0	2	6
Riddel, James	0	1	6	Walker, Samul	0	2	0
Riddel, James, Jun'r	0	2	0	Woods, John	0	3	0
Roger, Catren	0	3	9	Wilson, Jams	0	2	0
Roger, John	0	1	9	Willson, Joseph	0	1	6
Roger, Adam	0	1	9	Woods, Andrew	0	3	6
Robison, Philip	0	1	0	Willson, Thomas	0	1	0
Ripeth, Josep	0	1	0	Walmer, Peter	0	3	0
Rogers, James	0	5	0	Wilams, James	0	3	6
Richar, Jacob	0	4	0	Wever, John	0	2	0
Robinson, Thomas	0	1	6	Willson, Jams	0	2	6
Read, Adam, Eqr'r	1	10	0	Watson, William	0	2	0
Ramberey, Christen	0	2	0	Young, Samul	0	1	0
Sterret, Samul	0	5	0	Young, William	0	15	0
Sherp, John	0	2	6	Young, John	0	8	0
Slowen, Archabel	0	3	6	Park, John	1	0	0
Slowan, Samul	0	3	0	Peticrue, Jams	1	0	0
Stuart, John	0	4	0	McMullen, Gorge	1	0	0
Stuart, James	0	10	0	McCluar, John	1	0	0
Stuart, Lazrus	0	2	6	Clark, William	1	0	0
Shever, Gorge	0	3	0	Shanklen, Gorge	1	0	0
Snodey, Mathew	0	2	0	Strean, David	1	0	0
Snodgras, Robert	0	5	6	Dermond, William	1	0	0
Snodgras, Joseph	0	3	0	Robinson, Samul	1	0	0
Strean, John	0	1	6	Hill, Robert	1	0	0
Smiley, John	0	3	0	Wilkon, John	1	0	0
Smiley, Gorge	0	3	0	Willson, Hugh	1	0	0
Shaw, Deniel	0	2	0	Willson, William	1	0	0
Stuart, Samul	0	5	0	Willson, Thomas	1	0	0
Stuart, John	0	1	6	Andrew, James	1	0	0
Swan, John	0	1	0	Andrew, James	1	0	0
Tod, James	0	2	6	McFarlen, John	1	0	0
Thompson, John	0	3	0				
Tagert, Jams	0	2	6	The Honorable propraitors			
Thompson, John	0	4	0	for 24538 acres of Land at			
Thorntown, William	0	2	0	½ peny sterling per acre,			
Thompison, William	0	2	6	amouts to £51 2 5 ster., and			
Trousdal, William	0	2	6	to Corrennce, according to			
Telor, Mathew	0	3	6	Act, £68 3 2.			
Thompson, John	0	1	6	To tax to the first 60000 £ at			
Tibens, John	0	1	0	8d. per £, to	1	13	0
Taylor, John	0	2	0	To the first 100000 £, at one			
Tibens, John	0	2	0	shilling per £, at	3	8	1
Tubs, John	0	3	6	And the second 100000 £ to			
Tubs, Jacob	0	3	6	1s. 6d. per £	5	1	1
Tittel, Gorge	0	3	6	And this presents tito	5	1	1
Thompson, William	0	2	0				
Willison, James	0	9	6	Total tax	£15	3	3
Willson, Hugh	0	7	6				

The above Assessment, to be Duely Examenet to be just, as wittnes my hand pr. me.

ROBERT WALLACE.
SAMUL STERRET, *Colecter.*

[Orthography carefully compared with the original.]

were often driven from their homes. Forts and stockades were built for defence, but murders and massacres frequently occurred. So greatly were the people harrassed that many left their farms and homes for safer regions. On June 6, 1759, we learn that Mr. Sankey, having received a call to a congregation in Virginia, and designing to remove there, applied for and received credentials from the Presbytery. His relation to the Hanover church as pastor seems to have been already dissolved. He removed to Virginia, accompanied by many of the Hanover congregation, about 1760. The main reason for going was to escape the incursions of the savages. He settled at Buffalo, joined the Hanover Presbytery of Virginia in 1760, and was appointed to preside at the opening of the Synod of Virginia in 1785. He lived to a good old age, respected by his people and his brethren in the ministry.

Mr. Sankey served Hanover church for twenty-one years, and though no further record is known of his ministry, it was evidently an acceptable one to the people, who kept him so long, and many of whom accompanied him when he left. This closed the first pastorate of Hanover church. After his dismissal during the year 1759 the church was supplied occasionally by Rev. Messrs. John Steel and John Elder.

1760. At a meeting of the Presbytery in 1760 Hanover asked for supplies, and also sought from the Synod candidates for their pulpit, with a view to settlement. In the year 1760 Rev. Messrs. Elder, Duffield, Roan and Williams occasionally preached for them. The church asked Presbytery to secure for them from the Presbytery of New Brunswick a further hearing of a *Mr. Carmichael*, and that if possible he be induced to join the Presbytery of Donegal. The services of Mr. Latta, of Philadelphia Presbytery, were also sought. These two men, with Mr. Williamson, seem to have preached for the church as candidates, but were not chosen to the pastorate.

1761. During the year 1761 Hanover was supplied mainly by Rev. Messrs. Roan, Tate, Elder, Beard and M'Mordie.

PASTORATE OF THE REV. ROBERT M'MORDIE.

1762. In 1762, in November, a call was made for the Rev. Robert M'Mordie, which he accepted. The congregation promised him eighty pounds for his temporal support, to be secured by bonds. Rev. Messrs. John Elder and Joseph Tate were appointed to install him on the fourth Sunday of November, 1762, Mr. Elder to preside.

No record of the installation is made, but it was doubtless carried out at the fixed time.

The congregation had been diminished somewhat by the removals to Virginia. The Old and New Light controversies still troubled the churches and caused dissensions and divisions in the congregations. In April a number of persons, names not given, supplicate the Presbytery for a dismissal from Hanover church, with liberty to join some neighboring congregation. The matter was discussed and deferred from year to year. In June of the same year Rev. Messrs. Robert M'Mordie, John Elder, John Steel, John Beard, Joseph Tate and Sampson Smith declined to sit in Presbytery because of contention and party spirit. They all belonged to the Old Light side of the controversy.

1764. It is evident that a part of the congregation of Hanover were on the New Light side of the conflict, for in October, 1764, several members of the congregation represent to Presbytery that they never consented to take Mr. M'Mordie for pastor; that said call was made out irregularly, and they now request that they may be allowed to join some other congregation, probably that of the Rev. John Roan, who was a New Light man. The matter was deferred.

1765. It came up again in February, 1765, when Mr. M'Mordie objected to the Presbytery taking any action in the case. The petitioners were, however, granted leave to go elsewhere and have their children baptized, though they were not to dissolve their connection with Hanover church. This did not end matters, and in April the Presbytery met at Hanover to consider the troubles in that church. Nothing was accomplished, and they met again in May.

In the same month of May the Synod dissolved the Presbytery, and the Presbytery of Carlisle was formed, consisting of the ministers and churches west of the Susquehanna. It lived, however, but a year and died, and the Presbytery of Donegal was restored to its original bounds, and met June 24 at Carlisle. The churches and ministers of Donegal Presbytery east of the Susquehanna were organized into the new Presbytery of Lancaster. Mr. M'Mordie, with Hanover church, belonged to this Presbytery. It, too, survived but a year. During this year, 1765–1766, the church of Hanover became vacant. No record of Mr. M'Mordie's resignation exists, but it was doubtless caused by the dissensions in his church. After his withdrawal the church continued in a distracted and enfeebled state.

For many years it depended entirely upon occasional supplies, having no settled pastor, and, so far as we can learn, seeking none.*

1772. †April 16 Rev. John Roan was directed to supply at Hanover, and to moderate a call for Mr. William Thom, and Mr. Thom

---

1769. * The signatures to a "Petition of the Inhabitants of Hanover Township against the Division of the said Township," dated February, 1769, perhaps furnishes a pretty fair list of the members of Hanover congregation at that period. The original orthography of the names is preserved :

Timothy Green,
Samuel Paterson,
Daniel Shaw,
James Hutchison,
James Low,
Patrick Machan,
David Fergusson,
Samuel Fergusson,
William Fergusson,
William Cooper,
John Cooper,
John Stewart,
James Finney,
James Irwin,
Thomas M'Millan,
George M'Millan,
James M'Millan,
John Shaw,
Richard Johnson,
Mathew Snodey,
James Johnson,
John M'Cory,
William Wright,
James Robertson,
Robert Humes,
Thomas Finney,
Martha Barnet,
William Moorhead,
William Cathcart,
Robert Porterfield,
Thomas Strain,
James Thompson,
John Thompson,
Thomas Meen,

Thomás M'Elhinney,
James M'Creight,
Samuel Sturgeon,
Robert Dermond,
John M'Quown,
Joseph Allen,
William Creain,
Anthony M'Creight,
Lazaruis Stewart,
James Pettycrew,
Alexander Sloan,
James Robinson,
Mathew Thornton,
Robert Sturgeon,
John Andrew,
Alex'r M'Cay,
James Todd, --
John Campbell,
James M'Creight, jr.,
Richard Crawford,
Robert Kirkwood,
John Sharp,
Adam Read,
John Grame,
James Willson,
James Wilson,
Samuel Allen,
Isaac Hannah,
Matthew Hannah,
William Ripet,
Samuel Hutchison,
Thomas Scott,
John Woods,
Robert Hutchison,

Joseph Hutchison,
John Hutchison,.
James Hamilton,
Alex'dr Robinson,
James M'Clanachan,
Joseph Hutchison, jr.,
Thomas Kenedy,
Robert Kenedy,
William Brown,
Joseph Barnet,
William M'Cluar,
William Brandon,
Joseph Wilson,
Andrew Walles,
Thomas M'Cluer,
James Rogers,
William Rogers,
William Young,
John Crawford,
James Crawford,
James Wilson,
Robert Wallace,
Robert Parks,
Joseph Parks,
Joseph Snodgrass,
Michel Vanlear,
William M'Cullouch,
James Dixon,
Samuel Brown,
Andrew Endsword,
John Gilkeson,
Brice Innis.

1771. † Twice was the congregation at Hanover greatly depleted. First by the exodus into Virginia of forty or fifty families, who settled in Hanover county, where their beloved pastor, Rev. Mr. Sankey, had located. Earnest efforts have been made to gather the names of these Hanoverians, but as yet fruitless. Second, by the adherents of Lazarus Stewart, who accompanied. him to Wyoming. The names of nearly all of these have been secured, and are as follows :

Capt. Lazarus Stewart,
Lt. Lazarus Stewart, jr.,
James Stewart,
Lazarus Young,
William Stewart,
Robert Young,
William Young,
Peter Kidd,

John Robinson,
Adam Harper,
John Poop,
Adam Stover,
Balzer Stogard,
Ludwig Shalman,
Joseph Neal,
John Stillie,

William Carpenter,
———— Aston,
George Mean,
Conrad Philip,
Jacob Folk,
Robert Kidd,
Adam Sharer,
Thomas French,

is appointed one of the supplies at Hanover.   On the 21st of May a call for Mr. Thom was presented in Presbytery, with a copy of a subscription paper of over one hundred pounds.   The call was put into his hands.   In the meantime Mr. Thom received other calls from Big Spring, Sherman's Valley and Alexandria, Va., and on October 15, 1772, accepted the latter.   For the next seven years, covering part of the period of the Revolutionary war, the Hanover church depended on occasional supplies.   The times tried men's souls. Men were called away to war.   The people were poor.

1779.   October 19, 1779, a call from Hanover for Mr. Joseph Henderson was presented at Presbytery and put into his hands.   They agreed to pay him yearly, if he accepted, the full quantity of *five hundred bushels of wheat.*   The call was declined, and supplies continued for two years longer, when, on the 20th of June, 1781, a call from Hanover to Rev. Matthew Woods was made out, in which they promise to pay him *six hundred bushels of wheat*, or a sum of *hard* money equivalent thereto, and also a gratuity of six hundred bushels.   The cause of these peculiar calls in grain was the greatly depreciated value of the Continental currency.   Mr. Woods accepted the call, and was ordained and installed over the Hanover congregation June 19, 1782.

PASTORATE OF REV. MATTHEW WOODS.

1782-84.   The pastorate of Mr. Woods was a brief one, and there remains no record of it beyond the fact that August, 19, 1784, he reported in the Presbytery that some disturbance had arisen in his congregation, occasioned by a Rev. Mr. Hindman, who was formerly on trial before Presbytery for some irregularities.   He asked the interposition of Presbytery, and a committee was appointed to attend to the matter, but in less than a month, on September 13, 1784, the *Rev. Matthew Woods died.*   A tombstone was erected to his memory in 1789 by the following subscribers:

	£. s. d.		£. s. d.
Robert Boale	7 , 6	Samuel Kearsley	7 6
Capt. Dan'l Bradley	7 6	Capt. Jas. M'Creight	7 6
Capt. Andrew Lee	7 6	John Robertson	7 6
Isaac Harrison	7 6	John M'Elhaney	5 0
William M'Farland	7 6	Thomas Bell	3 9

Thomas Robinson,	Peter Izenhower,	Casper Riker,
John Simpson,	John Neal,	John Soult,
Peter Leaman,	John M'Downer,	Ronemus Haine,
Matthew Hollebaugh,	Luke Showley,	Martin Coster.
Jacob Stogard,	John Lard,	
George Ely,	Nicholas Fanning,	

	£.	s.	d.		£.	s.	d.
John Endsworth		7	6	Patrick Preston		3	9
Henry Graham..............		7	6	John Snodgrass		3	9
James Young, Sr.............		7	6	John Cooper...................		5	0
William Robertson...........		3	9	Robt. Fleming		3	9
William Stuart..............		3	9	Capt. Jas. Wilson		7	6
Wm. Brown and ten others in that quarter					1	9	0
James M'Clure and others in that quarter					1	17	3

The whole amount raised was.................................... 9 8 9

The body of Mr. Woods was buried in the Hanover grave-yard, adjoining the church.

1786. There was now a vacancy in the pastorate, during which supplies were furnished by Presbytery. After two years a call was extended to Mr. Samuel Wilson, a young licentiate, and a salary of £150 was promised him, but it was declined.

1787. Hanover was allowed to prosecute a call to a probationer for the ministry under the care of the Presbytery of Philadelphia. On the 16th of October *Mr. James Snodgrass* was received under the care of the Presbytery from the Philadelphia Presbytery, and having accepted a call from the Hanover congregation, he was appointed to prepare a lecture on Rom. VIII, 1-7, and a Presbyterial exercise on I Cor. XV, 22, as parts of his trial for ordination,

1788. On the 13th of May the Presbytery of Carlisle met at Hanover. Present—Rev. Messrs. John Elder, John Hoge, John Linn, John Craighead, Robert Cooper and Samuel Waugh, with James Johnston, elder. Upon the next day, May 14, 1788, James Snodgrass was ordained and installed as pastor of the Hanover congregation. Rev. John Craighead presided and gave the charge, and the Rev. John Linn preached the sermon from II Cor. IV, 5.

PASTORATE OF REV. JAMES SNODGRASS.

A copy of the call of Hanover church to Mr. Snodgrass:

SIR:—We the members of the Presbyterian congregation of Hanover, in the county of Dauphin, being for some time past destitute of a stated Gospel minister, and being sensible of the great loss that we and our tender offspring do sustain by our living in such a destitute condition in this wilderness, and being satisfied of the ministerial abilities of you, the Rev. James Snodgrass, do unanimously invite and call upon you to take the pastoral care and oversight of us, promising all due subjection, submission and obedience to the doctrine, discipline, government and ordinances exercised and administered by you as our pastor in the Lord. And that you may be better able to attend upon your pastoral and ministerial work, without anxious and distracting cares about your worldly concerns, we do hereby cheerfully promise and engage to provide for your support in a decent and comfortable manner, suitable and becoming your respectable office and station as a minister of the Gospel and Ambassador of the Prince of Peace, knowing that the Lord hath ordained that they who preach the Gospel shall live by the Gospel.

In testimony whereof, we hereby subscribe our names this tenth day of May, 1787.

JAMES M'CLURE,	WILLIAM CRAWFORD,
DAVID RAMSEY,	JAMES TODD,
SAMUEL STURGEON,	WIDOW BROWN,
ANDREW YOUNG,	DAVID FERGUSON,
JOHN SNODGRASS,	ISAAC HARRISON,
WILLIAM WILSON,	JOHN YOUNG,
RICHARD DE ARMAND,	HUGH ANDREWS,
JAMES M'CREIGHT,	JAMES DIXON,
DANIEL BRADLEY,	JOSEPH BARNET,
ROBT. PORTERFIELD,	THOMAS KENNEDY,
DAVID TODD,	JOHN M'COWN,
WILLIAM BROWN,	JAS. ROBERTSON,
THOMAS MURRAY,	ROBT. FLEMING,
THOMAS M'CHESNEY,	SAM'L KEARSLEY,
DAVID ROBERTSON,	JOHN TODD,
WILLIAM ROGERS,	JEREMIAH ROGERS,
ROBERT BOAL,	RICHARD CRAWFORD,
JOHN ROBISON,	JOSEPH CRAIN,
ANDREW KARR,	ISABELLA LOW,
JOHN M'CORD,	JAS. ROBERTSON,
WM. M'ELHENY,	WIDOW BEARD,
JOSEPH ALLEN,	WILLIAM CRAWFORD,
SAMUEL ROBINSON,	GEORGE WARD,
WILLIAM CATHCART,	JAMES JOHNSTON,

ROBERT M'FARLAND.

Contrary to modern custom the amount of the salary is not mentioned in the call, but from the book of the trustees, which is in existence, we learn that the amount of the salary was probably one hundred and fifty pounds. In subsequent years Mr. Snodgrass lived upon a farm near the church, of which he was the owner. The church, probably, owned no ground beyond a few acres surrounding the church, part of which was used as a burial ground. Mr. Snodgrass was the last pastor of Hanover, but he served the church through a very long pastorate, down to the day of his death, on the second day of July, 1846, a period of over fifty-eight years from the date of his installation, May 14, 1788. To this should be added the six months or more in which he supplied the pulpit prior to his ordination. The congregation of Hanover was wholly a country one, made up of a farming people and the few mechanics always to be found in a farming region. As the country increased in population the original Scotch-Irish settlers slowly disappeared, selling their farms to Germans and going themselves, mainly westward. Mr. Snodgrass, like most of the early ministers, failed to keep a record of his times. There does not exist, so far as can be learned, the slightest record of any church-session, or of any election of ruling elders by the church. Tradition gives us the names of some who served in the eldership of the church, but there is no existing record of any meeting of the session. No sessional book appears to have been kept. During the first eight or ten years of his pastorate Mr. Snodgrass kept in a blank book of the trustees of the church, a record of the marriages, baptisms and admissions to the church, but he seems to have become weary of it and to have utterly abandoned it before the year 1800. There is no record of removals from the church by letter or by death. A list remains of the heads of families about the year 1788, and the lists of those who paid stipends are continued down to the date of his death. Mr. Snodgrass' receipts for his salary, and the records of the board of trustees are also in existence. Some of these are here given, that they may be preserved for future reference.

NAMES OF HEADS OF FAMILIES ABOUT THE YEAR 1788.

Allen Joseph,	Dalton Robert,	Kennedy Thomas,
Andrew James,	Dixon Richard,	Long James,
Andrew John,	Dixon Sankey,	Low Widow,
Allen William,	Dearmond Richard,	M'Creight Anthony,
Bell Thomas,	Endsworth John,	M'Elheny John,
Barnet Margaret,	Espy Josiah,	M'Cullough Wm.,
Brown William Esq.,	Ewing Robert,	M'Cord John,
Barnet Joseph,	Finney Thomas,	M'Guire Joseph,
Barnet John,	French John,	M'Cullough Wm.,
Brandon William,	Fleming Robert,	M'Elheny Thomas,
Boal Robert,	Finley Richard,	M'Creight James,
Barnet Joseph,	Ferguson John,	M'Clure James,
Broadly Daniel,	Graham James,	M'Nitt Barnet,
Byers James,	Green Timothy,	M'Quown John,
Baird Widow,	Graham John,	M'Elheny William,
Brown Samuel,	Green Joseph,	Meskimmins Wm.,
Brown John,	Graham William,	Petticrew David,
Crain George,	Harrison Isaac,	Petticrew James,
Crane Joseph,	Hume Robert,	Pinkerton James,
Crane Ambrose,	Hume John,	Porterfield Robert,
Cunningham Patrick,	Hill Widow,	Ramage John.
Campbell Widow,	Innis Elizabeth,	Robertson James,
Crawford Richard,	Israelow Edward,	Robertson James,
Cathcart William,	Johnston James,	Rambo Peter,
Craig John,	Kearsley Samuel,	Rogers William,
Cooper John,	Kennedy Robert,	Rogers Jeremiah,
Crawford Elizabeth,	Kerr Andrew,	Ramsey David,

Robinson John,
Robinson Samuel,
Ray David,
Snodgrass John,
Sturgeon Samuel,
Strain David,
Swan Moses,
Strain Robert,
Stewart James,

Sturgeon Robt.,
Stewart Francis,
Snoddy Widow,
Todd James,
Todd John,
Todd David,
Thomson John,
Van Lier Michael,
Wilson James Sr.,

Wilson James Jr.,
Ward George,
Wallace Benjamin,
Wallace Andrew,
Wilson William,
Wallis Thomas,
Young Andrew,
Young James,
Young William.

This number, 108, shows that there was quite a good sized congregation in Hanover at that time.

HANOVER MARRIAGE RECORD.

The following is the register of marriages by Rev. James Snodgrass, so far as recorded:

A. D. 1788.

NAMES.		DATE.
John Barnett and	Jane Crane,	June 3.
Andrew Wilson and	Martha M'Clure,	June 5.
William Crane and	Mary Sawyer,	June 24.
Henry Graham and	Elizabeth Ferguson,	June 24.
Joseph M'Bay and	Jane Brown,	July 8.
Bernard M'Nitt and	Jane Hue,	August 14.
John M. Gilchrist and	Eleanor Berryhill,	October 28.
John M'Kesic and	Jane Israelow,	November 25.
George Green and	Lettice Ramsey,	December 18.

A. D. 1789.

James George and	Mary M'Clure,	January 13.
Walter Clark and	Mary Cathcart,	January 20.
Robert Stewart and	Sarah Finney,	March 10.
Henry M'Cormick and	Jane Mitchell,	June 15.
Robert Patterson and	Isabella Brisben,	June 23.
William Sturgeon and	Jane M'Ewen,	December 1.
John Smith and	Elizabeth Robertson,	December 22.

A. D. 1790.

Andrew Robison and	Jane Crane,	January 21.
William Allen and	Nancy Ainsworth,	March 18.
Charles Riddle and	Mary Beard,	March 23.
William Fleming and	Ann Stone,	March 25.
Charles Brown and	Margaret Allen,	March 25.
Thomas Barnett and	Jane Finney,	April 27.
John Beard and	Jane Cathcart,	August 12.
John Bay and	Hannah Cashity,	August 16.
David Ritchie and	Agnes M'Cormick,	September —.
William M'Clure and	Agnes Lewis,	November 30.
David Craig and	Martha Cook,	December 1.
Andrew Crane and	Jane Strain,	December 20.
Robert Starrett and	Rosannah Green,	December 30.

A. D. 1791.

James Finney and	Sarah Stewart,	February 14.
William Hays and	Elizabeth Mitchell,	March 1.
Patrick Dougherty and	Mary Quigley,	March —.
Samuel M'Clery and	Mary Young,	April 7.
Henry Fulton and	Ann Bell,	April 20.
John Craig and	Jennet Boyd,	September 2.
Moses Barnett and	Martha Snodgrass,	December 15.
Adam Bell and	Jane Robertson,	December 30.

NAMES.	A. D. 1792.	DATE.
John Chambers and	Mary Duncan,	January 24.
Henry Moor and	Mary Robertson,	February 2.
James Crane and	Margaret M'Clure,	March 18.
Thomas Moorhead and	Ann Clark,	March 15.
John Sloan and	Elizabeth French,	March 27.
William Beard and	Mary Boyd,	March 29.
John M'Callen and	Margaret Geddis,	April 10.
William Cathcart and	Abigail Hill,	May 1.
Hugh Wilson and	Ann Crawford,	May 10.
Samuel Ainsworth and	Margaret M'Ewen,	May 10.
Samuel Fulton and	Mary Hay,	May 29.
David Strain and	Elizabeth Allen,	October —.
James Burlin and	Frances Rogers,	November —.
Thomas Morrison and	Agnes Minsker.	
—— Stewart and	Sarah Stewart,	December 20.
John Byers and	Elizabeth Andrew.	

	A. D. 1793.	
Jeremiah Sturgeon and	Ann Ritchie,	March 14.
Samuel Elder and	Margaret Espy,	March 14.
Hugh Stewart and	Mary Wilson,	March 21.
John Carson and	Elizabeth Snodey,	April 2.
Daniel M'Guire and	Sarah M'Clure,	June —.
Joseph Laughead and	Elizabeth Brown.	
William Ward and	Mary Harrison,	October 31.
Samuel Moor and	Jane M'Clure,	November 19.
John M'Ewen and	Margaret Bradley,	November 28.

	A. D. 1794.	
Alexander Wood and	Mary Robison,	January 2.
Joseph Allen and	Eleanor M'Ewen,	May 8.

	A. D. 1799.	
William Sawyers and	Esther Rogers,	December 25.

	A. D. 1800.	
Hugh Andrews and	Elizabeth Ainsworth,	January 2.
William Wilson and	Jane Stewart,	February 11.
William Jackson and	Jane Black,	February 20.
William Stewart and	Mary Stewart,	March 13.
Benjamin Chambers and	Grace Stewart,	March 17.

The record of marriages here ends, though Mr. Snodgrass lived on in Hanover until July 2, 1846. He was born July 23, 1768, and was nearly 83 years old at the time of his death.

[THE LATER HANOVER MARRIAGES WHICH FOLLOW ARE COLLECTED FROM VARIOUS SOURCES.]

NAMES.	A. D. 1796.	DATE.
Harbison, Adam, and	Martha Finney,	April 14.
Isett, Henry, and	Frances Rodgers,	April 14.
M'Ewen, James, and	Frances Boal,	April 20.
Brice, Alexander, and	{ Peggy Kearsley, (Capt. Samuel,)	{ May 19.

	A. D. 1798.	
Galbraith, Bertram, and	Harriet Huling,	February 15.

	A. D. 1799.	
Sloan, Robert, (Harrisburg,) and	{ Sarah M'Cormick,	March 30.

3

NAMES.	**A. D. 1800.**	DATE.
M'Creight, John, and	Peggy Rowan,	January 1.
	A. D. 1802.	
Moody, Rev. John, and	Elizabeth Crawford,	March 30.
Moorhead, Mr., and	Ann Wilson,	March 30.
Stewart, Mr., and	Polly Stewart,	March 30.
Hayes, David, and	Margaret Rodgers,	December 21.
	A. D. 1803.	
Boal, Major Jacob, and	Mrs. George Crain,	January 27.
Wilson, James, and	Polly Wallace,	April 21.
Harrison, Isaac, jr., and	Nancy Crain,	April 27.
Wallace, William, (Harrisburg,) and	Rachel Forrest, (Dr. Andrew Forrest,)	April 27.
Hines, James, and	Love Clark,	August 10.
Crain, Jeremiah, and	Ann Cochran,	November 3.
	A. D. 1804.	
Rodgers, Robert, and	Effy Allen,	February 16.
Hill, Robert, and	Polly Todd,	February 20.
Green, Capt. Innis, and	Rebecca Murray, (Col. John.)	April 19.
Harrison, John, and	Frances Rodgers,	April 26.
M'Creight, John, and	Polly Dearmond,	November 15.
	A. D. 1805.	
Glenn, William, and	Jenny Andrews,	January 3.
Lytle, Major John, and	Elizabeth Green, (Col. Timothy,)	January 10.
Bell, Samuel, and	Isabella Watt,	February 14.
	A. D. 1806.	
M'Cullough, Alex., and	Jane Robinson,	December 24.
	A. D. 1807.	
Hamilton, Hugh, (Harrisburg,) and	Rosanna Boyd, (Adam Boyd,)	January 6.
Johnson, David, and	Eleanor Barnett, (Maj. John,)	February 18.
Bell, Thomas, and	Mary M'Chesney,	February 26.
Clark, John, and	Jane Simonton, (Dr. William,)	April 9.
Simonton, James, and	Anne Bell,	April 9.
Thome, John, and	Nancy Robinson,	April 16.
Robinson, Samuel, and	Rachel Clendenin,	June 19.
M'Elrath, John, and	Mary M'Cabe,	August 11.
Rodgers, John, and	Dinah Carson,	October 31.
Crawford, William, and	Patty Crain,	November 2.
Johnston, John, and	Ann Bradley,	November 2.
	A. D. 1808.	
Patton, Dr. William, (Hummelstown,) and	Eleanor Kean, (Gen. John Kean,)	March 24.
Kerr, Rev. William, and	Mary Wilson,	April 28.
Stewart, Samuel, and	Elizabeth Elder,	October 11.
Ryan, John, and	Lydia Stewart,	November 24.
	A. D. 1809.	
Sawyer, John, and	Miss Bell, (da. Sam'l,)	May 25.
	A. D. 1810.	
Sloan, James, and	Ann M'Creight,	March 29.
Stewart, James, and	Mrs. Hannah Wilson,	April 3.
Crawford, James, and	Mary Finney,	April 26.
	A. D. 1811.	
Bell, Rev. Samuel, and	Mary Snodgrass,	January 15.
Barnett, George, and	Maria Winnagle,	January 17.
Stewart, James, and	Jane Elder,	March 28.

A. D. 1813.

NAME.		DATE.
Barnett, Joseph, and	Elizabeth Allen,	March 30.
Hanna, John, and	Louisa Wilson,	April 9.
Miller, Robert, and	Eliza Dearmond,	April 11.
Johnson, Samuel, and	Ann Barnett,	April 20.
Gilchrist, Robert, and	Jane Young, (Wm.,)	October 28.

A. D. 1815.

Freckleton, Robert, and	Martha Humes,	December 26.
Todd, David and	Sarah M'Cormick,	May 23.

A. D. 1816.

Thom, William, and	Margaret Hays,	January 14.
Brenneman, Henry, and	Mrs. John Smith,	March 19.
Gilchrist, Robert, (Washington county,) and	Jane Fleming, (Sam'l,)	March 12.
Graham, John, and	Jane Ferguson, (David)	March 14.
Moorhead, Capt. John B., &	Ann Snodgrass,	May 1.
Forster, John, (Susquehanna twp.,) and	Mary Wilson,	October 1.
Espy, David, and	Rebecca Allen,	December 15.

A. D. 1817.

Snodgrass, Benjamin, and	Ann Wilson,	June 9.
Barnett, William, and	Ann Graham,	December 12.

A. D. 1818.

Dale, James, (Union county,) and	Eliza Bell,	February 24.
Sturgeon, Allen, and	Eliza Snodgrass, (Rev. James Snodgrass,)	March 5.
Sturgeon, Jeremiah, and	Mary M'Cormick, (John,)	June 25.

A. D. 1821.

Vanderslice, John, and	Mrs. Rosanna Boal,	January 5.

A. D. 1822.

M'Clelland, John, and	Sarah Stewart,	May 2.

A. D. 1826.

Sturgeon Robert, and	Eliza Ann M'Cormick,	April 13.
M'Cormick, Thos. M., and	Rebecca Rodgers,	December 14.
Geddis, William F., and	Nancy M'Cormick,	February 22.
Lutz, Henry H., and	Jane Barnett,	April 25.

REGISTER OF BIRTHS AND BAPTISMS.

A. D. 1788.

NAMES.	PARENTS.	BIRTH.	BAPTISM.
George Washington,	Daniel and Mary Bradley,	Dec. 20, 1787,	May 18
Alexander,	John and Elizabeth Martin,	January 15,	May 18
James,	Isaac and Sarah Harrison,	Nov. 12, 1787,	May 18
Ann,	William and Mary Graham,		May 18
Mary,	John and Mary Ramage,		May 18
Eleanor,	John and Mary Barnett,		May 25
Thomas,	David and Susanna Mitchell,	February 25,	May 25
Juliana,	William and Mary Stewart,	Aug. 5, 1787,	June 12
Jane,	William and Rebekah M'Farland,		June 12
Elizabeth,	William and Rebekah M'Farland,		June 12
Nancy,	James and Jane Caldwell,		June 15
David English,	James and Rachel Montgomery,		June 15
Alexander,	James and Mary Johnston,		June 15

NAMES.	PARENTS.	BIRTH.	BAPTISM.
Eleanor,	Richard and Eleanor Dearmond,	April 17,	June 15
Margaret,	John and Sarah M'Cord,	May 8,	June 15
Samuel,	James and Jane Clokey,	Apr. 24, 1787,	June 22
Alexander,	James and Jennet M'Creight,	July 2,	Aug. 10
Jane,	William and Martha Young,	June 1,	Aug. 17
Hannah,	James and Ann Wilson,	May 15,	Aug. 24
Elizabeth,	James and Ann Long,	May 23,	Sept. 14
Andrew,	Andrew and Sarah Young,		Sept. 14
John,	Samuel and Sarah Kearsley,	Septem. 14,	Sept. 19
James Snodgrass,	Joseph and Ann Espy,	July 18,	Sept. 25
John,	John and Agnes Young,	August 14,	Sept. 24
Mary,	Samuel and Nancy Stewart,	February 29,	Oct. 26
Jennet,	Robert and Martha M'Farland,		Oct. 28
William,	William and Hannah Calhoun,		Nov. 9
Matty,	Robert and Else Porterfield,		Nov. 30
Alexander,	John and Rebekah Martin,		Nov. 30
Mary,	John and Mary Hume,		Nov. 30

A. D. 1789.

Hugh,	James and Mary Todd,	January 10,	Mar. 1
James,	Andrew and Priscilla Lee,	January 3,	Mar. 13
John,	Samuel and Ann Finney,		April 5
Sally,	David and Barbara Stewart,		April 5
James,	Samuel and Rebekah Brown,		April 5
Ephia,	Joseph and Sarah Green,		April 27
James Snodgrass,	Robert and Jane Sturgeon,		April 27
John,	Hugh and Mary Graham,	April 10,	May 3
Mary,	James and Elizabeth Wilson,		May 3
Joseph,	John and Jane Barnett,		May 31
Mary,	William and Mary Crane,		May 31
Robert,	William and Elizabeth M'Elheny,	April 13,	June 28
Mary,	Joseph and Mary Riddle,	May 3, 1782,	June 2
Rebekah,	Joseph and Mary Riddle,	Sept. 9, 1785,	June 2
Margaret,	Joseph and Mary Riddle,	Mar. 2, 1788,	June 2
John,	Henry and Elizabeth Graham,	April 17,	June 14
Robert,	William and Agnes Cunningham,	May 15, 1784,	June 15
Sarah,	William and Agnes Cunningham,	Feb. 2, 1786,	June 15
William Norris,	William and Agnes Cunningham,	Mar. 16, 1788,	June 15
Joseph,	George and Martha Crane,	July 1,	July 19
Elizabeth,	William and Rebekah Allen,		July 26
Martha,	Andrew and Catharine Carr,		Aug. 16
Jennet M'Kroy,			Aug. 16
Mary,	Andrew and Jane Martin,		Aug. 19
Mary,	Thomas and Mary Erskine,	Dec. 2, 1788,	Aug. 19
Sarah,	Bernard and Jane M'Nitt,		Aug. 23
Mary,	Jeremiah and Mary Rogers,		Aug. 23
Martha,	Robert and Elizabeth Strain,		Sept. 6
Margaret,	Robert and —— Freckleton,		Sept. 6
John,	Sankey and Ann Dixon,	August 14,	Sept. 25
James,	William and Martha Young,	Septem. 14,	Oct. 11
Benjamin,	James and Martha Snodgrass,	August 15,	Oct. 17
George,	Thomas and Mary Ward,	Septem. 5,	Oct. 18
James,	William and Margaret Campbell,	Septem. 14,	Nov. 8
Sally,	John and Mary Low,		Nov. 15
Joseph,	John and Mary Barnett,		Nov. 22
David,	David and Barbara Stewart,		Nov. 29
Martha,	Andrew and Martha Wilson,		Dec. 6
Elizabeth,	David and Jane Ferguson,		Dec. 20
Ellen M'Millan,			Dec. 20
Jane,	Francis and Eleanor M'Clellan,		June 14

A. D. 1790.

David,	William and Hannah Calhoun,	Oct. 4, 1789,	Jan. 3
Sarah,	James and Jane Clokey,		Jan. 17
John,	Samuel and Margaret Sturgeon,	January 6,	Feb. 10

NAMES.	PARENTS.	BIRTH.	BAPTISM.
Sarah,	John and Jane Cooper,	Dec. 21, 1789,	Feb. 10
Richard,	Timothy and Mary Green,	January 8,	Feb. 11
Ann,	Samuel and Sarah Kearsley,	January 13,	Feb. 21
Rebekah,	John and Elizabeth Martin,	Dec. 1, 1789,	Feb. 21
James,	John and Mary Snodgrass,	Dec. 14, 1789,	Feb. 28
Robert,	Robert and Mary Boal,	February 23,	Mar. 10
Margaret,	Andrew and Margary Young,	Nov. 16, 1789,	Mar. 10
Sarah,	John and Rebekah Martin,	Oct. 26, 1789,	Mar. 10
Mary Ann,	John and Margaret M'Elheny,	January 26,	Mar. 12
Mary,	John and Mary Magill,		April 2
Robert Scott,	Adult,		April 4
Samuel,	John and Mary Elder,		April 25
Richard,	William and Jane Rogers,		April 25
William,	James and Mary Johnston,		April 30
William,	James and Rachel Montgomery,		May 3
Margaret Roan,	John and Jane Barnett,	March 23,	May 3
Mary,	David and Susanna Mitchell,	January 16,	May 3
Matilda,	James and Ann Long,	March 28,	June 6
Sarah,	Isaac and Sarah Harrison,		June 6
Elizabeth,	James and Jane Caldwell,		June 20
Sarah,	James and Jane Caldwell,		June 20
James,	John and Elizabeth Petticrue,	January 25,	June 20
Agnes Crain,	Robert and Sarah Stewart,		June 20
Mary,	Robert and Ann Kirkwood,		June 27
James,	John and Jane Robison,		July 4
Josiah,	Andrew and Sarah Young,		July 11
Sally,	Henry and Jane M'Cormick,	June 15,	Aug. 5
Frances,	David and Mary Bradley,	July 29,	Aug. 16
Isabella,	William and Mary Snodey.		
James,	John and Sarah M'Cord.		
Isabella,	Hugh and Agnes Andrew,	Septem. 29,	Dec. 4
John M'Cown,	William and Jane Sturgeon,		Dec. 5

A. D. 1791.

NAMES.	PARENTS.	BIRTH.	BAPTISM.
William,	William and Elizabeth M'Elheny	Nov. 21, 1790,	Jan. 2
John,	John and Mary Hume,	Oct. 4, 1790,	Jan. 30
Samuel,	John and Mary Petticrue,		Jan. 30
James,	Charles and Margaret Brown,	January 18,	Mar. 2
Martha,	Joseph and Jane M'Bay,	Nov. 29, 1790,	Mar. 2
Andrew Stewart,	Richard and Eleanor Dearmond,		Mar. –
Samuel Allen,	James and —— Barnett,		April –
Jean,	Henry and Elizabeth Graham,	Oct. 19, 1790,	April –
David,	James and Mary Todd,		May 1
Nancy,	John and —— Beatty,		May 1
	John and Agnes Young,		April 27
Esther Morrow,			May 1
Elizabeth Guerney,	Adult,		May 13
John,	Thomas and Mary Ward,		May 16
Esther,	William and Martha Young,	April 16,	May 19
Susanna Louisa,	Lewis and Margaret Kreider,	March 24,	May 19
David,	David and Jane Ferguson,		May 29
Thomas,	James and —— Wilson,	April 14,	May 31
James M'Cord,			May 31
David Grahms,			May 31
	William and Ann Fleming,		July –
	Robert and Else Porterfield,		July –
Timothy Green,	William and Rebekah Allen,		July 11
John,	William and —— M'Cullough,		July 11
Samuel,	Samuel and Rebekah Brown,		July 31
Joseph Crane,	William and Sarah Knox,		Sept. –
Robert,	Robert and Jane Sturgeon,		Oct. 2
Thomas Kittera,	Benjamin and Rebekah Duncan,		Oct. 12
Jane Maria,	Benjamin and Rebekah Duncan,		Oct. 12
John M'Ewen,	John and Mary Barnett,	Septem. 7,	Oct. 30
William Sawyer,	William and Mary Crane,		Nov. 6

NAMES.	PARENTS.	BIRTH.	BAPTISM.
Elizabeth,	Samuel and Ann Finney,		Nov.
Martha,	William and Margaret Campbell,		Nov. 9
Isaac,	John and Rebekah Martin,	Septem.	5, Nov. 9
Mary S.,	James and —— Armstrong,		Nov. –

A. D. 1792.

Martha,	James and Martha Snodgrass,	Nov. 25, 1791,	Jan. 11
Andrew Lee,	George and Martha Crane,		Jan. 11
Samuel,	William and Nancy Allen,		Feb. 3
Susanna,	Robert and Sarah Stewart,		Feb. 1
William,	Andrew and Catharine Carr,		Feb. 15
Mary,	Thomas and Jane Barnett,	Nov. 25, 1791,	Feb. 15
John,	James and Jane Caldwell,		Mar. 7
David,	David and Susanna Mitchell,		Mar. 14
Samuel,	James and Ann Long,		Mar. 14
Samuel,	Robert and —— Aitkin,		Mar. 25
John,	Robert and Martha M'Farland,		April 15
James,	William and —— Petticrue,		April 15

ADMISSIONS TO THE LORD'S TABLE.

Samuel Stewart	Nov. 2, 1788	Patrick Preston	1790
Nancy Stewart	Nov. 2, 1788	John Barnet	1790
David Mitchell	Nov. 2, 1788	Joseph Crain	1790
Violet Crawford	Nov. 2, 1788	James Crain	1791
Elizabeth Miskimins	Nov. 2, 1788	Alex. M'Elheny	1791
John Andrew	Apr. 26, 1789	Henry M'Cormick	1791
Jane M'Ewen	Apr. 26, 1789	Jane M'Cormick	1791
Eleanor M'Ewen	Apr. 26, 1789	Wm. Cathcart	1791
Samuel Brown	Apr. 26, 1789	Elizabeth Sloan	1791
Mary Beard	Apr. 26, 1789	Benjamin Duncan	1791
Martha Wilson	Apr. 26, 1789	Jean Flenegan	1791
Hannah M'Elheny	Apr. 26, 1789	Margaret M'Ewen	1791
Thomas M'Elheny	Apr. 26, 1789	Jeremiah Sturgeon	1791
Abbe Hill	Apr. 26, 1789	Mary Robison	1791
Hugh Graham	Apr. 26, 1789	Wm. M'Farland	May, 1792
Mary Snodey	Apr. 26, 1789	Rebekah M'Farland	May, 1792
John Hume	Apr. 26, 1789	Wm. Beard	May, 1792
Mary Hume	Apr. 26, 1789	Samuel Ainsworth	May, 1792
Jane Crane	Apr. 26, 1789	Hugh Wilson	May, 1792
Jane Bell	Apr. 26, 1789	John M'Cown	May, 1792
William Stewart	May 2, 1790	—— Wray	May, 1792
Hugh Andrew	May 2, 1790	John Sloan	Oct., 1793
John Crawford	1790	Elizabeth Sloan	Oct., 1793
Ann Crawford	1790	Thomas Barnett	Oct., 1793
William Crane	1790	Jane Barnett	Oct., 1793
Samuel Finney	1790	Moses Barnett	Oct., 1793
Ann Finney	1790	Martha Barnett	Oct., 1793
John Robinson	1790	John Robison	Oct., 1793
Wm. Sturgeon	1790	Martha Crawford	Oct., 1793
Elizabeth Lewis	1790	Jane Sloan	Oct., 1793

CONTRIBUTORS AND MEMBERS OF HANOVER CONGREGATION FROM 1787 TO 1842.

A.

Allen, Joseph	1787–1818	Allen, William	1790–1793
Allen, William	1787–1830	Allen, Joseph, jr	1795–1838
Andrew, James	1787–1793	Ainsworth, Samuel	1795–1797
Andrew, John	1787	Allen, Rebecca	1796–1804
Ainsworth, John	1788–1812	Ainsworth, Lazarus	1796–1802
Andrew, Hugh	1788–1803	Ainsworth, James	1797–1803
Atkin, Robert	1790–1793	Adams, John	1799–1801
		Allen, John	1802–1809

Allen, Robert 1803-1823
Allen, James 1806-1821
Auston, Mrs 1808-1809
Allen, John 1813-1823
Ainsworth, Widow 1813-1827
Allen, Miss 1839-1842

B.

Baird, Widow 1787
Barnett, Capt. John 1787-1795
Barnett, Joseph 1787-1796
Barnett, Margaret 1787-1788
Brandon, Wm 1787
Brown, John 1787
Brown, Samuel 1787-1817
Brown, Wm., sr 1787-1807
Broadley, Daniel 1787-1802
Boal, Robert 1787-1811
Byers, James 1787-1803
Bell, Thomas 1787-1815
Baird, John 1788-1789
Barnett, James 1788-1804
Barnett, Widow 1789
Barnett, Thomas 1789-1830
Brown, Charles 1790-1800
Baird, Sarah .'........... 1790-1793
Bell, Henry 1790-1793
Barnett, John 1790-1822
Beard, William 1795-1806
Barnett, Moses 1797-1815
Bigham, James 1797-1798
Bigham, Joseph 1799-1803
Brown, Thomas 1799-1842
Brail, John 1802-1803
Bell, James 1802-1839
Barr, Alexander 1802-1803
Boyd, Mrs 1804-1807
Bell, Alexander 1805-1831
Barnett, Widow 1805-1812
Boal, Thomas 1806-1811
Baird, Widow 1807-1832
Boon, John 1808-1815
Barnett, Joseph 1813
Barnett, Samuel 1813
Bell, Widow 1816-1820
Barnett, Richard 1820-1826
Baker, Samuel 1823
Barnett, William 1823-1830
Beel, Jacob 1826-1827
Barnett, Thomas, jr 1831-1842
Barnett, Richard 1831-1832
Beard, Mrs., (estate) 1833
Bell, James, (estate) 1840-1841
Barnett, Thomas, (estate).. 1836
Beard, William 1834-1838
Beard, J 1837-1838
Barnett, John 1837-1842
Bell, Robert 1842

C.

Campbell, Widow 1787
Cathcart, Wm., sr 1787-1796
Cooper, John 1787-1793
Craig, John 1787
Crain, George 1787-1795
Crane, Ambrose 1787-1792
Crane, Joseph 1787-1789

Crawford, Elizabeth 1787
Crawford, Richard 1787-1813
Cunningham, Patrick 1787-1789
Clokey, James 1788-1813
Crawford, Wm 1788-1811
Caldwell, James 1788-1791
Carson, William 1788-1789
Campbell, Margaret 1788-1804
Campbell, Wm 1788-1803
Crain, Andrew 1790-1796
Crain, William 1790-1795
Crain, James 1793
Campbell, Robert 1796-1798
Carson, Francis 1796-1798
Cathcart, Wm., jr 1796-1831
Crain, Martha 1796-1803
Cathcart, Widow Sarah.... 1797-1801
Crawford, Paul 1797-1800
Crawford, John 1797-1812
Cathcart, James 1802-1815
Clokey, Joseph 1802-1815
Campbell, More 1804
Campbell, Widow 1804-1813
Connelly, Moore 1803-1806
Carr, Mrs 1806-1810
Crain, Jeremiah 1806-1808
Carr, Samuel 1811-1817
Corbett, James 1811-1827
Crawford, Miss 1813-1842
Cathcart, Widow 1816-1835
Cuppler, James 1820-1831
Corbett, Mrs 1828-1842
Crawford, V 1831-1837
Cowden, John 1841-1842

D.

Dalton, Robert 1787-1806
Dearmond, Richard 1787-1802
Dixon, Richard 1787
Dixon, Sankey 1787-1790
Dixon, James 1788-1823
Duncan, Benjamin 1791-1796
Dearmond, Eleanor........ 1803-1827
Dougherty, George 1806-1809
Douglas, Joseph 1790
Dalton, Thomas 1807
Dalton, Anna 1807
Drummond, Frances....... 1813-1817
Dixon, Ann 1815
Dixon, Miria 1815
Duey, Thomas 1831-1836
Duey, George 1831-1834

E.

Endsworth, John 1787
Espy, Josiah 1787
Ewing, Robert 1787-1789
Elder, John 1790-1812
Ewin, (Ewing,) John 1791-1797
Erskine, Thomas 1797-1799
England, Moses 1802-1809
Elder, Robert 1810-1812
Ewens, Thomas 1811

F.

Ferguson, John 1787-1813
Finlay, Richard 1787-1795
Finney, Thomas 1787-1818

Fleming, Robert........... 1787-1818
French, John 1787
Ferguson, David........... 1788-1842
Finney, Samuel 1788-1824
Finney, Widow........... 1789-1800
Freckleton, Robert 1796-1829
Finney, John 1796-1811
Finney, Mary, and sisters.. 1801-1805
Finney, Jean, and sisters.. 1803
French, James............. 1803-1842
Ferguson, Sarah 1804
Fleming, Samuel 1813-1842
Forster, John............. 1819-1820
Fleming, Mrs............ .. 1819-1842
Finney, Mrs 1825-1842
Fleming, Samuel B....... 1827-1842

G.

Graham, James............ 1787
Graham, John 1787-1792
Graham, William.......... 1787-1788
Green, Joseph 1787-1797
Green, Timothy........ ... 1787-1804
Graham, Henry........ ... 1788-1801
Gurney, Nancy 1791-1796
Gurney, Eliza............. 1791-1800
Graham, Widow 1793
Graham, Hugh 1795-1821
Gurney, Elizabeth 1796-1798
Gillespy, James........... 1798-1811
Graham, John 1820-1823
Graham, Moses 1825
Graham, Hugh, jr 1825-1831

H.

Harrison, Isaac 1787-1804
Hill, Widow.............. 1787
Hume, John.............. 1787-1798
Hume, Robert 1787
Hume, John 1790-1797
Hillis, William........... 1795-1799
Hill, John 1797-1809
Hill, Robert 1797-1842
Hume, Isabella........... 1799-1816
Hume, Martha........... 1799-1815
Harrison, John 1805-1836
Hampton, John........... 1811-1833
Hatton, Frederick 1813-1834
Harrison, Steven 1814-1821
Hatton, Daniel........... 1815-1823
Hume, John......... 1817-1821
Hall, John 1819-1821
Harrison, Mrs 1822-1827
Hatton, Mrs.............. 1835-1840
Harrison, Mrs............ 1836-1838
Harrison, Andrew 1837-1840
Harrison, John, (estate)... 1837

I.

Innes, Elizabeth........... 1787
Israelow, Edward.......... 1787-1797
Innes, Brice 1791-1796
Innis, Mrs 1812-1827
Innis, John B............. 1828-1831

J.

Johnston, James........... 1787-1811
Jude, Samuel.............. 1787-1802

Johnston, John 1804-1811
Johnston, Rowan 1804-1831
Johnston, James 1804-1809
Johnston, William........ 1808-1811
Johnston, Samuel 1812-1819

K.

Kearsley, Samuel.......... 1787-1795
Kennedy, Robert 1787-1811
Kennedy, Thomas......... 1787-1801
Kerr, Andrew 1787-1795
Kirkwood, Robert 1793-1795
King, John 1799-1802
Kee, John 1799-1810
Kell, Benjamin 1802-1810
Kennedy, Jean 1802-1803
Kerr, Mrs 1804-1805
Kell, Aaron.............. 1807-1819
Kell, John............... 1808-1809
Kirk, James 1823-1835

L.

Long, James.............. 1787-1789
Low, Widow............. 1787-1795
Lee, Capt. Andrew 1788-1797
Lewis, Robert 1792-1798
Low, George.............. 1797-1802
Low, Ned................ 1798
Latta, John 1812-1813

M.

M'Clure, James............ 1787-1816
M'Creight, Anthony....... 1787
M'Creight, James.......... 1787-1814
M'Cord, John............. 1787-1811
M'Cullough, Wm.......... 1787
M'Elhany, John........... 1787-1808
M'Elhany, Wm........... 1787-1790
M'Guire, Joseph 1787
M'Nitt, Barnett........... 1787-1819
M'Cown, John............. 1787-1805
Miskimins, Wm 1787-1791
M'Elhaney, Thomas....... 1787-1820
M'Farland, Wm 1788-1798
M'Elhaney, Alex.......... 1788-1811
M'Cormick, Wm 1789-1795
Martin, John 1789-1815
Montgomery, James....... 1790-1792
M'Farlin, Robert 1790-1792
M'Millen, James........... 1790
Mitchel, Thomas........... 1790-1801
Mitchel, David............ 1790-1811
M'Cormick, Henry 1790-1824
M'Cullough, Hugh 1790-1791
M'Clelland, Francis....... 1790-1793
M'Ewen, John............ 1791-1798
M'Coy, Thomas............ 1791-1792
M'Cormick, Isabel......... 1791-1799
Martin, Andrew 1793-1805
M'Kinney, Esther 1795-1803
Morrow, Archibald 1796
M'Clelland, John.......... 1796-1800
M'Bay, Joseph............ 1796-1815
Murray, Archibald 1797-1804
M'Candless, William 1797-1799
M'Ewen, James 1797-1800
M'Naughton, John 1798-1805

M'Cune, James	1799–1803	Porterfield, James	1821–1824
M'Cormick, John	1800–1811	Poor, Charles M	1824–1825
M'Clure, Francis	1802–1808	Porterfield, James	1829–1842
M'Clure, John	1802–1813	Porterfield, Robert	1831–1835
M'Creight, David	1802–1840	—— estate	1835–1836
M'Elheny, Robert	1803–1811	Porterfield, Mrs	1837–1838
Mathews, Thomas	1803–1804		
M'Clurg, Wm	1803–1829	**R.**	
M'Mese, Robert	1803–1812	Ramage, John	1787–1793
M'Roberts, Hannah	1804–1812	Rambo, Peter	1787
Moody, Robert	1804–1809	Ramsey, David	1787
M'Creight, John	1804–1811	Ray, (or Wray,) David	1787–1803
M'Clurg, Robert	1804	Robertson, James	1787–1793
M'Cormick, Wm	1805–1809	Robinson, John, sr	1787–1806
Moor, William	1805–1808	Robinson, Samuel	1787–1802
Martin, Widow	1806–1828	Rogers, William	1787–1800
M'Ewen, John	1806–1810	Rogers, Jeremiah	1787–1788
M'Neight, Alex	1806–1810	Robertson, David	1788–1790
M'Neight, John	1806–1811	Ramsey, Lettice	1788
Murray, Andrew	1806–1823	Robertson, James	1790–1791
M'Mullin, Daniel	1807–1812	Rigart, John	1791–1801
M'Nair, Thomas,	1807–1826	Robeson, Widow	1793–1795
M'Veay, Joseph	1807	Richey, David	1793–1823
M'Fadden, John	1808–1809	Roan, James	1796–1803
M'Henry, Archy	1808	Roan, Matthew	1796–1803
M'Clure, Widow	1808–1818	Robeson, Robert	1796–1800
M'Connell, Wm	1808–1827	Rogers, Jean	1801–1807
M'Twig, (or Taig,) John	1812–1819	Robinson, Widow	1801
M'Creight, Mrs. E	1813–1837	Ramsey, James	1802–1832
Mulholland, James	1813–1822	Robinson, John, jr	1804–1819
M'Kinnis, Wm	1813–1814	Rogers, Robert	1804–1836
M'Creight, Alex	1815–1840	Rogers, James	1806–1818
M'Bay, Wm. B	1816–1837	Rogers, William	1808
M'Clure, Andrew	1817–1823	Robinson, Samuel	1810–1830
M'Clure, John	1819–1826	Robinson, Thomas	1813–1825
M'Nitt, Sarah	1820–1822	Ralston, William	1821–1823
M'Elhenny, John	1821–1842	Ramsey, James, (estate,)	1833
M'Neel, Curtis	1824–1826	Ramsey, Mrs	1834–1836
Martin, James	1821–1835	Robinson, Moses	1837–1842
M'Farland, Mrs	1821–1823		
M'Creight, James	1822–1825	**S.**	
M'Clennan, Matthew	1822–1823	Snodgrass, John	1787–1817
M'Hargue, Alexander	1824–1827	Snody, Widow	1787
M'Cormick, Mitchel	1825–1842	Stewart, Francis	1787–1790
M'Creight, Mrs	1826–1842	Stewart, James	1787
M'Farland, Wm	1829–1830	Strain, David	1787
M'Connell, James	1830–1835	Strain, Robert	1787–1793
M'Bay, Mrs	1838–1841	Sturgeon, Robert, sr.	1787–1804
M'Cord, Samuel	1840–1842	Sturgeon, Samuel	1787–1801
		Swan, Moses	1787–1793
N.		Stewart, William	1788–1807
Norris, Charles	1791–1792	Sloan, Alexander	1788–1812
		Strain, Elizabeth	1789–1827
O.		Stewart, Robert	1790–1842
Ogden, Hiram	1814	Snody, William	1790–1812
		Stewart, Samuel	1790–1803
P.		Smith, William, sr	1790–1801
Pettycrew, David	1787	Sloan, Archibald	1790–1793
Pettycrew, James	1787–1792	Stewart, John	1791–1802
Pinkerton, James	1787	Simpson, James	1791–1799
Porterfield, Robert	1787–1828	Sturgeon, William	1791–1792
Pettycrew, John	1788–1792	Sloan, John	1793–1833
Prentice, James	1799–1802	Sturgeon, Jeremiah	1796–1826
Pinkerton, Hugh	1802–1803	Smith, William, jr	1796–1800
Peterson, James	1807–1810	Sturgeon, Thomas	1799–1800
Pecock, James	1811	Sturgeon, Robert, jr	1799–1801
Porterfield, Robert, jr	1817–1823	Small, John	1801–1803

Smith, Francis	1802–1811
Smith, John	1802–1819
Sturgeon, Margaret	1802–1819
Smith, Nancy	1803
Stewart, Widow	1804–1813
Snodgrass, Wm	1804–1809
Sloan, James	1806–1820
Snodgrass, Samuel	1806–1834
Sister, John	1805
Sister, Thomas	1805
Sister, Daniel	1807–1809
Sturgeon, Samuel	1809–1820
Sturgeon, Widow	1805–1819
Snodgrass, John, jr	1810–1830
Stewart, Miss F.	1811–1813
Snody, Widow	1813–1827
Sturgeon, Joseph	1813–1815
Sloan, William	1813–1823
Sturgeon, Widow	1816–1829
Stewart, James	1816–1823
Snodgrass, Thomas	1817–1830
Snodgrass, Benjamin	1818–1842
Smith, Widow	
Sturgeon, Allen	1820–1842
Snodgrass, Robert	1820–1840
Sloan, Mrs	1821–1836
Simonton, Wm	1825–1842
Stephen, John J	1825
Sturgeon, Mrs	1827
Snodgrass, James	1835–1842
Sloan, Alex	1837–1838

T.

Thomson, John	1787–1811
Todd, David	1787–1803
Todd, James	1787–1793
Todd, John	1787–1832
Todd, Mary	1795–1802
Thom, William	1802–1842
Thom, John	1802–1815
Thomson, John	1802–1829
Todd, Widow Anna	1804–1828
Todd, James	1804–1840
Todd, Widow Mary	1811–1813
Todd, David	1814–1842
Todd, Samuel	1814–1840

V.

Vanlier, Michael	1787–1800
Vance, Martha	1792–1807

Vanlier, Widow	1801–1812
Vanderslice, Dr. John	1827–1840
Vanderslice, Mrs	1841–1842

W.

Wallace, Andrew	1787
Wallace, Benjamin	1787–1792
Ward, George	1787–1802
Wilson, James, sr	1787–1819
Wilson, James, esq	1787–1807
Wilson, William	1787–1796
Ward, Thomas	1788–1803
Wallace, Widow	1788–1797
Wilson, Andrew	1790–1806
Wallace, William	1793–1798
Wright, John	1799–1802
Waugh, Alex. M	1799–1810
Wilson, Samuel	1804–1806
Wilson, Moses	1806–1807
Wilson, Widow	1806–1810
Wilson, Joseph	1806–1817
Wilson, Mrs. Andrew	1807–1814
Wilson, James, jr	1807–1815
Witmere, Philip	1808–1809
Wilson, Moses	1813–1825
Wilson, Samuel	1814–1822
Wilson, Joseph	1814–1826
Wilson, Mrs	1820–1837
Wilson, Mrs. A., (estate)	1815–1817
Ward, Isaac	1821–1823
Walker, Samuel	1824–1827
Wilson, Mrs., (estate)	1838
Wilson, Misses	1839–1842

Y.

Young, William	1787–1795
Young, Andrew, sr	1787–1801
Young, James, sr	1787–1801
Young, John, sr	1788–1801
Young, John, jr	1788–1796
Young, Andrew, jr	1788–1824
Young, Martha	1796–1816
Young, James	1797
Young, George	1808–1814
Young, Mrs	1825–1840
Young, Misses	1827–1838

Z.

Zuber, Jacob	1820

At a meeting of the congregation held April 6, 1797, "agreable to a notice from the pulpit on Sunday, a vote was taken to know in what manner the money should be raised to compleat the grave-yard wall of said corporation of Hanover. It was carried by a majority that the congregation should be sest agreable to the duplicates of the county tax for this year, and that James M'Creight, William Wilson and John Todd are appointed sessors for the same."

ASSESSMENT.

	£. s. d.		£. s. d.
Allen, James	2 15 0	M'Creight, James, esq	4 2 6
Allen, Robert	1 13 0	Martin, Andrew	1 6 6
Allen, Joseph	1 13 0	M'Ewen, John	2 9 3
Allen, William	2 6 3	M'Nitt, Barnard	2 9 6
Ainsworth, James	0 4 6	M'Clure, James	3 6 0
Allen, Widow	0 8 5	M'Cormick, William	1 4 3
Andrew, Hugh	5 10 0	M'Cormick, Henry	1 5 3
Ainsworth, John	2 15 0	M'Elheny, Thomas	3 6 0
Brown, Samuel	2 9 6	M'Cord, John	1 13 0
Baird, Wm	1 19 1	M'Ewen, James	2 9 6
Barnett, James	2 6 9	M'Bay, Joseph	0 7 1
Brown, William	2 13 0	M'Elheny, John	2 13 0
Brown, Charles	1 16 4	Martin, John	0 11 0
Barnett, Moses	2 6 3	M'Farland, William	3 6 0
Barnett, John	1 15 3	Porterfield, Robert	2 12 3
Barnett, Thomas	1 10 3	Robinson, Samuel	1 15 9
Bradley, Daniel, esq	3 6 0	Rogers, William	3 0 6
Boal, Robert	4 19 0	Robertson, Robert	2 11 10
Bell, Robert	0 16 6	Ramsey, James	1 13 0
Byers, James	2 4 0	Swan, Moses	2 6 3
Bell, Thomas	3 11 6	Stewart, Robert	1 11 0
Clokey, James	1 2 0	Sturgeon, Samuel	3 12 9
Cathcart, James	3 0 6	Snoddy, William	1 14 8
Crain, Widow	3 0 6	Strain, Widow	1 2 0
Crawford, John	3 1 9	Sloan, Alexander	3 15 0
Crawford, Wm	3 17 0	Snodgrass, John	4 8 0
Cathcart, Wm	1 2 0	Snodgrass, Rev. James	— — —
Campbell, Wm	2 15 0	Sturgeon, Jeremiah	1 11 0
Campbell, John	0 5 6	Sturgeon, Robert	4 19 0
Dearmond, Richard	4 19 0	Sloan, John	1 13 0
Dixon, James	2 7 11	Stewart, Wm	3 11 0
French, James	2 7 11	Stewart, John	1 13 0
Ferguson, David	6 14 3	Todd, David	3 0 6
Do. in trust	2 14 1	Todd, John	7 14 0
Ex'r Crain estate	2 9 6	Todd, Widow	4 12 6
Finney, Samuel	2 12 3	Thomson, John	3 6 0
Finney, Widow	2 3 0	Ward, George	1 16 4
Freckleton, Robert	2 3 0	Wilson, James	4 19 0
Finlier, Michael	1 18 6	Wilson, William	2 14 3
Fleming, Robert	3 6 0	Wallace, Benjamin, esq	3 6 0
Finley, Richard	0 16 6	Wilson, James, esq	4 19 0
Finney, John	2 2 0	Wilson, Andrew	3 2 9
Graham, Hugh	4 19 0	Ward, Thomas	1 9 7
Green, Timothy, esq	8 16 0	Young, Andrew	2 4 0
Graham, Henry	3 6 0	Young, James	2 4 0
Hume, John	2 18 4	Young, Widow	3 4 6
Hill, John	2 19 6	Young, James, jr	1 13 0
Harrison, Isaac	5 10 0	Young, Andrew, jr	2 1 3
Johnston, James	2 15 0	Robinson, John	7 3 0
Kennedy, Thomas	2 9 6	Stewart, Samuel	3 6 0
Kennedy, Robert	2 2 0	Rogers, James	3 0 6
Low, James	1 7 6	Bell, Samuel	2 9 6
Lee, Andrew	3 6 0	Snodgrass, Wm	2 16 1

Whole amount assessed on the congregation was............... 293 16 2

The following description of Mr. Snodgrass is given by his son, the Rev. Dr. W. D. Snodgrass, of Goshen, N. Y.:

In person my father was about 5 feet 11 inches in height. His

frame was erect, strong and in every respect well developed. His
hair was dark and changed to an iron-gray, though it never became
white, even in his last years. He was of a pleasant countenance
and amiable disposition, remarkably free from anything calculated
to incur the dislike or displeasure of those with whom he had inter-
course, fond of society, animated in conversation, and in every way
agreeable to all around him. His bodily health during the greater
part of his life was almost uninterrupted. He was temperate, sim-
ple and regular in his mode of living, and for years in succession
was not absent from his pulpit a single day on account of sickness.
As a preacher he had by nature the advantage of a good voice. He
spoke distinctly, was animated and earnest, and drew the matter of
his discourses directly from the Bible. During a considerable portion of ministry his Sabbath morning exercise was in the form of
an exposition or lecture. He selected a book generally from the
New Testament, and commented upon it from beginning to end, selecting larger or smaller passages as his judgment dictated, and
closing with extended practical remarks. He was clear, logical and
forcible in his statements of truth, and was regarded by his ministerial brethren, who knew him best, as an able, impressive and profit-
able preacher."

Rev. Wm. Simonton, his grandson, who knew him only in his
later years, gives the following as his impression of him thirty-one
years after death: "I only remember him as an old man, with sil-
very hair, and stooped with age. He was of medium height and of
a little more than medium weight. His complexion was light, his
features regular, except the end of the nose, which was somewhat
prominent and inclined upward; with a mild and pleasant expression of countenance. The color of his eyes I cannot with certainty
recall, but I think they were gray."

"He always preached memoriter. His sermons were written very
compactly, in a kind of short-hand, in which the vowels were omit-
ted. When committing them he paced the room. They were me-
thodical, clear, scriptural, spiritual and evangelical. Father once
remarked that he had 'never heard grandfather use an ungrammat-
ical expression in the pulpit.' He was discriminating and accurate
in his statements, and in the delivery of his discourses he never
hesitated or recalled a word. His voice and enunciation were good,
though he used but a few notes of the scale. There was not, therefore, as much variety in his tones as is desirable in a public speaker.

His manner was solemn and impressive. His gestures, as I remember them, were confined for the most part to the hands, which peered out of very long coat-sleeves. The gestures were made with the fore-arm resting upon the Bible or pulpit. His 'principal prayer' was long, systematic and comprehensive. It embraced the parts of prayer given in the Directory for Worship, Chap. V, and generally in the order there observed. He believed in the Divine control of nature's operations, and in times of drought he prayed for 'seasonable and refreshing showers.' Nor did he omit to give thanks for the same when the hopes of the husbandman were filled."

"I remember hearing him say that punctuality ought to have a place among the cardinal virtues. He exemplified these virtues by beginning the services from ten to five minutes before the appointed time. This was his habit. He took a deep interest in public affairs, and entered heartily into conversation upon the topics of the day, but habitually interjected serious reflections and suggested a spiritual improvement of the subject without interrupting the flow of thought or turning it into a channel distinctly religious. He had a very happy faculty of this kind. He used it with effect in impressing the minds of the young and without giving offence to any class of the thoughtless and indifferent. In this respect his conduct came nearer to that of the ideal minister than that of any I have ever known."

RULING ELDERS OF OLD HANOVER.

[SO FAR AS WE HAVE BEEN ABLE TO ASCERTAIN THEM.]

Lazarus Stewart, 1735,	Robert Boal,	Samuel Sturgeon,
Robert Grier, 1738,	James Wilson,	Henry M'Cormick,
John Cunningham, 1738,	Brice Innes,	Thomas M. M'Cormick,
Thomas Bell,	David Ritchie,	John M'Ilheny,
James Johnson,	James Todd,	Robert Fleming,
William Brown,	Robert Sloan, Senior,	

Mr. Snodgrass lived in Hanover until his death, which occurred July 2, 1846. He was a man of energy and decision. German settlers gradually bought up the farms. It was related to the writer by the Rev. Dr. Wm. R. DeWitt, that at one time during Mr. Snodgrass' ministry he was elected township constable. Some of the new-coming settlers were altering their road-lines, contracting the highway. Probably Mr. Snodgrass objected. In contempt and ridicule, not believing he would serve, the people chose him constable. They were mistaken. He at once qualified, appointed a deputy, who went through the township and compelled every offender to re-set his fences upon the right lines.

The church was very weak at the time of his death and never had another pastor. The building fell into decay, and was at length, in 1875 or '76, taken down. The care of the Glebe funds and the cemetery grounds was placed in the hands of trustees. But three church members remain in 1877. They will probably be transferred to Paxtang church, and the Hanover church be stricken from the roll of Presbytery.

HANOVER CHURCH BURIAL RECORD.

[The following list of deaths has been copied from the tomb-stones in the Old Hanover grave-yard, except those marked with an asterisk (*), which have been collated from other sources:]

NAME.	WHEN BORN.	WHEN DIED.
Ainsworth, John,	1740,	Aug. 14, 1812
Ainsworth, Margaret, w. Jno.,	1744,	Sept. 13, 1828
Allen, Eleanor, w. Jos.,	1769,	Feb. 1, 1834
Allen, Elizabeth, w. Wm.,	Mar., 1705,	May 3, 1800
*Allen, Jane, w. Jos.,	1729,	Aug. 7, 1804
Allen, Jean,	1801,	Aug. 27, 1812
*Allen, Joseph,	—	1817
Allen, Joseph,	Jan. 25, 1769,	Oct. 1, 1839
Allen, Mary, d. Wm. and N.,	1802,	July 4, 1822
Allen, Nancy,	1766,	Jan. 2, 1845
Allen, William,	Feb., 1709,	Dec. 23, 1784
Allen, Col. William,	1744,	Oct. 16, 1794
Allen, William,	1766,	Nov. 14, 1844
Andrews, Ann, w. Hugh,	1768,	May 1, 1797
Andrews, James,	1734,	May 7, 1784
Andrews, Jane, w. Robert,	1731,	June 17, 1787
Andrews, Dr. John,	1766,	Jan. 5, 1793
Barnett, Jane,	Dec. 22, 1769,	May 9, 1830
Barnett, John,	1751,	Sept. 2, 1797
Barnett, John,	Aug. 18, 1752,	May 5, 1823
Barnett, John,	1772,	1817
*Barnett, Mary, w. Moses,	—	June 10, 1802
Barnett, Mary,	Sept. 9, 1762,	Mar. 10, 1806
Barnett, Mary, d. Wm. Montgomery,		
Barnett, Martha, (Snodgrass,)	1773,	June 1, 1802
Barnett, Susanna,	1796,	Mar. 7, 1762
Barnett, Thomas, sr.,	Nov. 13, 1761,	Mar. 28, 1836
Barnett, Thomas, jr.,	1794,	Mar. 13, 1858
Bell, Ann, w. Thos.	1744,	Sept. 18, 1804
Bell, Catharine, w. Jas.,	1782,	Oct. 1, 1826
Bell, James,	1772,	Mar. 6, 1841
Bell, Mary, w. Thos.,	1758,	Aug. 11, 1820
Bell, Thomas,	1737,	June 23, 1815
Boal, Frances,	1751,	Aug. 27, 1779
Boal, Mary, w. Robert,	1756,	Aug. 22, 1804
Branden, James,	1771,	Sept. 6, 1804
Byers, James,	1746,	Sept. 8, 1804
Byers, John,	1751,	Jan. 12, 1797
Campbell, John,	1732,	June 1, 1781
*Campbell, Capt. Wm.,	—	July 3, 1804
Cathcart, Abby, w. Wm.,	1770,	June 1, 1825
Cathcart, James,	1772,	Apr. 27, 1816
Cathcart, Sarah, w. Wm.,	1737,	Sept. 25, 1804
Cathcart, William, sen.,	May 2, 1728,	Jan. 8, 1797
Craig, John, k. by the Indians,		Oct. 22, 1756
Craig, Isabel, w. John, k. by the Indians,		Oct. 22, 1756
Clokey, Mary,	Mar., 1794,	Oct. 13, 1799
Crain, George,	1739,	May 12, 1796

NAME.	WHEN BORN.	WHEN DIED.
Crain, Jean,	1705,	Feb. 15, 1753
Crain, Mary,	1736,	Apr. 8, 1789
*Crawford, John,	1780,	Feb. 18, 1811
Culbertson, Ann, [aged 72 years.]		
Davis, Martha, w. Wm.,	1728,	May 7, 1793
Dearmond, Eleanor, w. Rd.,	May 4, 1753,	Feb. 19, 1830
Dearmond, James, s. Rd.,	Oct. 2, 1782,	Jan. 7, 1812
Dearmond, Margaret,	Mar. 1, 1793,	May 6, 1824
Dearmond, Richard,	Sept. 1, 1743,	Nov. 17, 1802
Dillon, Nancy,	1760,	Aug. 30, 1850
Dixon, Ann,	1786,	Feb. 3, 1848
Dixon, James,	1708,	Sept. 19, 1782
Dixon, James,	1804,	Jan. 20, 1824
Fleming, Margaret, w. Rob't,	1734,	Dec. 13, 1813
Fleming, Mary, w. Samuel B.,	1806,	Nov. 10, 1836
Fleming, Capt. Robert,	1737,	Feb. 4, 1817
Fleming, Samuel,	1761,	Aug. 3, 1851
Fleming, Samuel B.,	1797,	Jan. 19, 1855
Fleming, Sarah, w. Sam'l,	Mar. 13, 1771,	Jan. 21, 1831
Fleming, Sarah, d. Sam'l,	Oct. 1, 1807,	July 13, 1828
Ferguson, Andrew, s. David,	1793,	Aug. 29, 1804
Ferguson, David,	1764,	Mar. 20, 1848
Ferguson, David,	June, 1791,	Aug. 18, 1793
Ferguson, Jane, w. David,	1753,	Nov. 18, 1824
*Ferguson, Sarah, w. John,	1760,	Aug. 5, 1823
Forster, Mary, w. Jno.,	1796,	Jan. 31, 1823
Freckleton, Margaret,	1757,	Apr. 10, 1824
French, Capt, James,	Jan. 26, 1777,	July 19, 1851
French, John,	1742,	Aug. 7, 1783
Graham, James,	1736,	Mar. 22, 1786
Graham, Jane, w. John,	Dec. 27, 1788,	Jan. 2, 1819
Green, Effy, w. Tim.,	1735,	Dec. 28, 1765
Green, Jean, w. Tim.,	1748,	Feb. 18, 1774
Grimes, Elizabeth, w. Sam'l,	1757,	Oct. 4, 1792
Hampton, John,	1761,	May 11, 1850
Hampton, Joseph A.,	1814,	Nov. 26, 1837
Hampton, Mary, w. Jno.,	1771,	Sept. 27, 1858
Hampton, Samuel,	1841,	June 2, 1865
Hampton, Samuel D.,	1808,	Aug. 21, 1837
Harrison, Francis, w. Jno.,	1781,	Apr. 15, 1813
Harrison, Isaac,	1744,	Jan. 31, 1806
Harrison, James,	1788,	Apr. 6, 1810
Harrison, Gen. John,	Jan. 8, 1775,	Feb. 28, 1837
Harrison, Rachel, w. Jno.,	1787,	Nov. 10, 1829
Harrison, Samuel,	1784,	Dec. 8, 1799
Harrison, Sarah, w. Isaac,	1748,	May 14, 1806
Harrison, Stephen,	1794,	July 31, 1821
Hatton, Frederick,	May, 1774,	June 3, 1835
Hatton, Mary, w. Fred.,	June 2, 1795,	July 7, 1840
Heaslet, Mary Ann,	1713,	July 18, 1796
Innis, Brice, sen.,	1711,	Feb. 18, 1778
Innis, Dr. Brice,	1751,	Jan. 6, 1778
Innis, Elizabeth, w. Brice,	1715,	Jan. 3, 1788
Kell, Elizabeth,	1750,	Feb. 6, 1805
*Kennedy, Thomas,	——	Jan., 1803
Kirk, Margaret, w. James,	1776,	June 5, 1831
Kunckleman, Jacob,	Feb. 13, 1769,	Feb. 20, 1820
Lingle, Daniel,	1795,	Dec. 31, 1865
Long, Martha, [defaced.]		

NAME.	WHEN BORN.	WHEN DIED.
M'Bay, Nancy, *w.* Wm.,	1790,	Feb. 16, 1845
M'Bay, William B.,	1792,	Sept. 27, 1837
M'Clure, Frances,	1778,	Jan. 23, 1809
M'Clure, James,	1733,	Nov. 14, 1805
M'Clure, James,	1780,	Sept. 10, 1815
M'Clure, John,	1781,	Aug. 22, 1827
M'Clure, Samuel,	Feb., 1814,	Mar. 14, 1839
M'Cormick, Henry,	1769,	Feb. 24, 1828
M'Cormick, Jane,	1764,	Aug. 6, 1844
*M'Cormick, William,	——	July, 1810
M'Cormick, William A., *s.* Thos. M.,	[Infant,]	Feb. 13, 1837
M'Creight, Elizabeth, *d.* Jas.,	1772,	Aug. 25, 1837
M'Creight, James, esq.,	1741,	Nov. 21, 1807
M'Creight, James, *s.* Jas.,	1778,	July 18, 1825
M'Creight, Jeannet, *w.* Jas.,	1751,	Sept. 13, 1828
M'Creight, Sarah, *d.* Jas.,	1795,	Oct. 26, 1811
M'Creight, William, *s.* Jas.,	1792,	Dec. 17, 1814
M'Elhenny, John,	Sept. 11, 1754,	June 25, 1806
M'Elhenny, Mary Ann,	Nov., 1770,	May 27, 1805
M'Elhenny, Mary,	1733,	Aug. 4, 1807
M'Elhenny, Thomas, sen.,	1745.	Sept. 1, 1829
M'Elhenny, Thomas,	Feb., 1777,	Aug. 19, 1839
M'El' 'nny, Thomas,	July 4, 1781,	June 27, 1868
M'Kin 'y, Esther, *w* Jno.,	1743,	Feb. 23, 1818
*M'Nai., Martha, (Sturgeon,)	1774,	Jan. 11, 1803
Palmer, Mary Ann, *d.* Jno.,	——	Mar. 6, 1798
Petticrew, David,	1713,	July 2, 1784
Porterfield, Ann,	1783,	Dec. 2, 1835
Porterfield, Gracey,	1784,	July 29, 1793
Porterfield, Elizabeth,	1793,	Nov., 1800
Porterfield, Elsie, *w.* Robert,	1763,	July 28, 1828
Porterfield, John M.,	1795,	Mar. 27, 1820
Porterfield, Robert, sen.,	1757,	Aug. 28, 1829
Porterfield, Robert,	1786,	June 22, 1836
Porterfield, Wallis,	1797,	May 11, 1822
Ramsey, David,	1745,	Sept. 18, 1787
Ramsey, James,	1773,	Apr. 27, 1833
Reed, Adam, esq.,	1703,	Feb. 2, 1769
Reed, Mary, *w.* A.,	1712,	June 11, 1783
Robertson, James,	1724,	Mar. 17, 1792
Robertson, Margaret, *w.* Wm.,	1723,	Mar. 3, 1775
Robertson, Sarah, *w.* Wm.,	1744,	Aug., 1781
Robertson, William,	——,	Feb. 9, 1794
Rogers, Andrew,	1746,	Sept. 19, 1782
Rogers, Andrew, *s.* Rob't,	Nov., 1806,	Feb. 26, 1835
Rogers, Effey, *w.* Rob't,	Oct., 1783,	Jan. 25, 1811
Rogers, Col. John,	——	Dec. 6, 1799
Rogers, James,	1735,	Apr. 18, 1790
Rogers, James, jr.,	1768,	May 16, 1823
Rogers, Martha, *w.* Jas., jr.,	1765,	Aug. 23, 1839
Rogers, Timothy, *s.* Rob't,	——,	Oct. 15, 1821
*Rogers, William,	——,	Oct., 1802
*Rogers, Jane, *w.* Wm.,	1754,	Mar. 29, 1822
Sawyer, John,	Oct. 25, 1772,	May 5, 1837
Scheil, John,	Jan. 17, 1802,	Aug. 25, 1822
*Simonton, John M.,	——	1825
*Simonton, Dr. William, sen.,	——	Apr. 24, 1800
Simonton, Dr. William,	1788,	May 17, 1846
Sloan, Alexander,	1785,	Jan. 11, 1812
Sloan, James,	1775,	Dec. 1, 1820
Sloan, Nancy, *w.* Jas.,	1785,	June 18, 1837
Snodgrass, Ann,	1749,	May 25, 1807
Snodgrass, Ann,	1797,	Jan. 14, 1842

NAME.	WHEN BORN.	WHEN DIED.
Snodgrass, Benjamin,	1731,	July 1, 1804
Snodgrass, Rev. James,	July 23, 1763,	July 2, 1846
Snodgrass, John,	1746,	Jan. 2, 1829
Snodgrass, John,	1787,	Jan. 20, 1806
Snodgrass, Martha, w. Rev. James,	Nov. 12, 1760,	Dec. 20, 1828
Snodgrass, Mary, w. Jno.,	1747,	Mar. 11, 1838
Snodgrass, Mary, w. Jno.,	1777,	Feb. 8, 1815
Snodgrass, Mary, d. Jno.,	1768,	Mar. 17, 1773
Snodgrass, Nancy, w. Rev. Jas.,	1770,	Jan. 24, 1839
Snodgrass, William,	1774,	Oct. 18, 1800
Snodgrass, William,	1746,	Aug. 6, 1811
Snodgrass, William, jr.,	——	Dec. 7, 1799
*Sterrett, John,	——	Nov., 1797
Stewart, Frances,	1720,	Nov. 16, 1790
Stewart, Mary, w. Wm.,	1736,	Feb. 22, 1780
Stewart, Martha, 2d w. Wm.,	1743,	Aug. 9, 1799
Stewart, William,	1738,	July 14, 1803
Stewart, Susan, d. Rob't,	1836,	May 13, 1856
*Stewart, Samuel,	——	Sept. 16, 1803
Sturgeon, Allen,	1795,	July 31, 1865
Sturgeon, Eliza, w. Allen,	1794,	Jan. 1, 1848
Sturgeon, Margaret, w. Sam'l,	1754,	Oct. 9, 1834
Sturgeon, Martha, d. Sam'l,	April, 1785,	Oct. 4, 1801
Sturgeon, Jane, w. Rob't,	1744,	Feb. 21, 1809
Sturgeon, Robert,	1739,	June 30, 1805
*Sturgeon, Samuel, sen.,	——	Jan., 1795
Sturgeon, Samuel,	1741,	Oct. 2, 1801
*Sturgeon, Mrs., w. Sam'l, sen.,	——	Sept. 20, 1803
Thorne, Margaret, w. Wm.,	1780,	Feb. 20, 1863
Thorne, William,	1777,	Oct. 16, 1848
Todd, Anne,	[Infant,]	May 30, 1795
Todd, David,	1751,	Nov. 9, 1803
Todd, Eli James,	1830,	Aug. 27, 1839
Todd, Hugh,	1788,	Dec. 16, 1809
Todd, James,	1748,	Sept. 14, 1794
Todd, James,	1804,	July 2, 1831
Todd, James Wilson,	1816,	Apr. 15, 1837
Todd, Mary,	1719,	Feb. 15, 1775
Todd, Mary,	1756,	Dec. 25, 1813
Todd, Mary, d. Dav.,	Nov., 1785,	Feb. 2, 1795
Todd, Sally,	1780,	Dec. 27, 1831
Todd, William,	[Infant,]	July 5, 1784
Todd, James,	1712,	Sept. 9, 1783
Todd, John,	1742,	Sept. 14, 1804
Vanderslice, Eleanor, w. Dr. Jno.,	Oct. 27, 1805,	Jan. 20, 1830
Vanderslice, Dr. John S.,	1801,	Sept. 23, 1841
Wilson, Andrew,	1759,	Sept. 11, 1806
*Wilson, Ann, w. Jas.,	1752,	Jan. 6, 1801
Wilson, Eliza,	July, 1802,	Aug. 18, 1817
Wilson, Isabella,	1792,	Sept. 20, 1812
Wilson, James,	1798,	Nov. 14, 1817
Wilson, Martha, w. And.,	1768,	Dec. 20, 1814
Wilson, Martha,	1789,	Nov. 18, 1811
*Wilson, Sally, d. Jas.,	1785,	Feb. 10, 1810
*Wilson, Samuel,	——	Oct. 9, 1823
Woods, Rev. Matthew,	1757,	Sept. 13, 1784
*Wallace, Gen. James,	——	Dec. 17, 1823
*Wallace, Benjamin, esq.,	——	Dec. 8, 1803
*Wallace, Rachel, w. Gen. James,	——	Feb. 15, 1823
Young, William,	——	1796

THE

Conewago Congregation

OF

PRESBYTERIANS,

Londonderry Township,

DAUPHIN COUNTY.

1730-1796

BY A. BOYD HAMILTON.

CONEWAGO CHURCH.

THIS narrative has no claim to originality, or to be of any special interest; yet the facts presented are too precious to be lost, and however void of general interest they may be found, are worth preserving in this permanent form. In a very few years all trace of the godly men who formed this congregation would have been lost, and the episode here preserved, is therefore worth examination, imperfectly as it is presented.

As early as July, 1718, there was a considerable population above the mouth of Conoy creek, in Chester, now Lancaster, county, on the east bank of the Susquehanna river. From 1720 to 1725 many of the restless spirits of it migrated further westward, mostly into the broad and well-watered valley of the Conewago creek, now the division line between the counties of Lancaster and Dauphin. These emigrants settled mainly along a road which in after days came to be the Harrisburg, Elizabethtown and Lancaster turnpike. The location nearly midway between Elizabethtown and Middletown. These settlers were emigrants from the Province of Ulster, Ireland. They were all of the Presbyterian faith, and having, as is supposed, erected a place of worship, began early in 1735 to agitate the question of a settled pastor. From that time, as we know, they were furnished with supplies by the Presbyteries of Newcastle and Donegal. In 1741 they subscribed a sufficient sum and were furnished with a permanent pastor.

As long ago as 1796 all trace of the position of the church building was obliterated from the face of the earth. No tradition or relic remains of it, notwithstanding very diligent inquiry has been made for information respecting its location. A ruinous burial place is all that is left of what was once an active congregation of Presbyterians, "amid a land of gushing springs."

Thus it has happened, that at the period when the researches relative to this extinct congregation were made, not a dozen persons in the county of Dauphin, except a very few in immediate vicinity to a couple of deserted burial places, knew enough about it to "point the spot where active men and women rested from all earthly toil an hundred years ago."

In 1877, as will be observed by the papers which are embodied, Rev. William A. West, pastor of the Westminster Presbyterian congregation at Harrisburg, received a letter from a clerical friend in North Carolina. To enable him to frame a reply to his correspondent, many inquiries were instituted, generally without success. It is the purpose of this sketch to present a brief narrative of the steps taken to obtain information respecting an historical fact, of which we were so ignorant.

The Rev. Dr. E. F. Rockwell writes:

COOL SPRINGS, IREDELL Co., N. C., *January 24,* 1877.

James Hall and wife, Prudence (Roddy) Hall, the parents of Rev. James Hall, D. D., who went to General Assembly sixteen times, and was wedded 1803, came here and settled on Fifth creek, near Bethany church, 1751-2. They had a certificate: "That James Hall and his wife Prudence (Roddy) Hall heath lived in this congrigation ever since it was erected, & heave behaved themselves cristianly & soberly without aney public scandal known to us, & heave been partakers of sealing ordinances amonghst us, & may be recived into aney cristian society wherever God in his Providence shall order their lott, is certified this 20t day of august 1751 by the session att Conawago.

THOMAS BOWMAN,   JOHN M'QUEEN,
ROBERT MORDAH,   JAS. MORDAH."
HUGH HALL,

We are desirous to know where and whether there is any record like this—any names yet remaining there like these? The first four are names of the Scotch-Irish settlers here from Pennsylvania about that time. These parties had a son Hugh Hall. We have found twenty-four or twenty-five ministers of the Gospel among the descendants of James and P. Hall, and about twenty-eight females have married preachers. Rev. Robert Hall, who died last November at Oxford, Ohio, was a grandson. They have spread out all over the country. I preach one-half of the time at Bethany church, which is the name of a post office near by, you may see on Colton's map (atlas.) We had our Centennial celebration August, 1875, and had a large assembly.

Last October I was in Philadelphia. I saw Rev. J. G. Craighead, D. D. He advised me to write to Rev. W. S. Van Cleave, Gettysburg. There was a church Conawago near there, but he replies that there are no such names on their records or tomb-stones; says that there is or *was* a church of that name in Dauphin county, organized earlier than his, and suggests that I write to you for information. I hope, therefore, that you will excuse me for troubling you with this matter. It is one of some historical interest.

In 1750 the people emigrated here, apparently in colonies, from Pennsylvania. The church of *Centre* in lower end of this, Iredell, county till 1753; *Anson* till 1788; *Rowan*, too, had a set of names, Davidson, Templeton, M'Pherson, Givens, &c. Next north, Fourth creek (now Statesville) had different names—Simonton, Allison, Stevenson, Hall, Mordah, &c. Bethany is a branch of Fourth creek. I am located ten miles from Statesville, and letters reach me either at S. or here, at Cool Springs.

Since the above was written I notice that Dr. Wm. H. Foster in Sketches North Carolina, states that Dr. James Hall was from Carlisle, Pa. I see in Minutes Gen. Ass. Pres. Carlisle, a church Great Conewago, Rev. Joseph Henderson pastor till 1795, when he is w. c. and the church vacant. Do. 1800. But after 1801 Rev. David M'Conaughy pastor. Whether the same I am inquiring for or not I have no means of knowing."

The minutes of the original Presbytery of Donegal were first consulted, and the following relating to this congregation was found:

June 28, 1738. The people of Conewago ask to be erected into a congregation by themselves. P. 237.

August 31, 1738. Terms of separation between the churches of Conewago and Derry. P. 244.

October 8, 1741. Geo. Davidson from Conewago presents to Presbytery a supplication and call for Mr. Black.

April 5, 1743; May 26, 1743, and September 6, 1743. The name of John M'Quown is found in the lists of Ruling Elders. The church represented is not mentioned.

April 4, 1745. Presbytery released Rev. Samuel Black from his pastoral charge at Conewago in order to send him to Virginia to labor.

September 4, 1745. Hugh Hall, commissioner from Conewago, appeared and asked that the relation between Mr. Black and them might be renewed.

September 25, 1745. The above request was granted.

With this much before us, a communication was addressed to the "Journal," at Middletown, Dauphin county. It appeared in that newspaper February, 1877. It brought a response from Samuel Evans, Esq., of Columbia, fixing the locality of the church near Mount Joy, Lancaster county, erected for Rev. John Roan in 1742; or if not that one, one in Adams county, now "Great Conewago."

The call of Rev. Samuel Black was in 1741. He probably had preached to this congregation previously, as he was in the neighborhood, preached at Carlisle, in 1736–37, and presided at the installation of Rev. John Elder at Derry and Paxtang churches in 1738. Upon inquiry it was found that Mr. Black never preached at " Great Conewago."

The question of locality was set at rest, by a communication signed " J. R." in a subsequent issue of the " Journal," in which he truly fixed the site of the church, *or its grave-yard*, about three-fourths of a mile in an eastern direction from GEINBURG—not " Gainesburg," as on the maps—formerly the village of Franklin. The exact location is upon the farm of Mr. J. Alwine, in Londonderry township.

" J. R," (Dr. Ringland, of Middletown,) shows conclusively the ownership of the spot belonging to this extinct organization. He says:

" The piece of ground belonging to the church was a portion of a larger tract, which was taken on a warrant bearing date the first day of August, 1743, granted to Samuel Clark by the Land Office. The land was afterwards patented to Robert Spear, by patent deed, November 8, 1785, and was called " Spear's Choice," and called for 202⅝ acres and the usual allowance. The patent was enrolled in Rolls Office, in Patent Book No. 4, page 99, &c. The following memorandum, accompanying a draft, will explain itself:

' Re-surveyed for Robert Spear, August 18, 1785, the above tract of land, containing two hundred and two acres and five-eighths and allowances, situate in Derry township, Dauphin county, late Lancaster, by warrant granted to James Clark, 28th of July, 1743.
' Signed   BARTRAM GALBRAITH.

' N. B. The above square piece of nineteen by twenty perches is a Presbyterian meeting house and burying-grounds.
' To JOHN LUKENS, S. G.
' Returned into the Land Office the third November, 1785, for John Lukens, Esq., S. G.

EDWARD LYNCH.'

" The piece of ground designated as the burying-ground contained somewhat more than two acres. A number of stones, placed to mark the graves of those buried there, are still standing, but many have been carried away and put to other uses. The stones are all undressed red sand stone, without date or any other inscription. The foundation walls of the building still remain, though in a some-

·what dilapidated condition. There is nothing on our county records to show when, by whom, or to whom the title for this piece was made.

"The church must have been a very small affair, as the foundation is only about twelve feet by sixteen. A portion of the ground was during the last summer planted in corn. 'Black-haw' and other trees are growing within the area of the church wall. Tradition has it, that the carpenter who built the church fell from the roof and was killed, and was the first person buried on the ground."

A personal examination of the site of the grave-yard was made in May, 1877, in company of Hon. John Blair Linn, of Bellefonte, Hon. Joseph H. Nisley, of Middletown, and Dr. William H. Egle, of Harrisburg. The enclosure which Dr. R. supposes to have been a church foundation is a dilapidated wall, enclosing the burial-place of some important families. There is no inscriptive stone to tell what it really was. It is about ten by twelve feet. Clearly there is no mark of a church at this spot. What is very remarkable, there is not a tomb-stone, or part of one, with any inscription in the mass of fragments of such memorials which surround the family enclosure spoken of. The stones are of the red sand stone of the neighboring hills—many of them buried in the earth as taken from the quarry, free from all evidence of manual adornment—weather-beaten as well as rough.

The small space set off for the congregation was part of the lands of Clark & M'Kee. This reservation was as early as 1737, before either of these members of the church had any legal claim to the land, but there was no adverse title, and the gift was a good one.

A warrant was granted 1742—a survey returned, excluding these two acres, in 1743. In 1785 it was again surveyed, and described as follows:

North 34″ west 19 perches.
South 56″ west 20 perches.
South 34″ east 19 perches.
North 56″ east 20 perches.

A great part of this plot was prepared for corn when our company examined it.

After searching all the early assessments of that portion of Dauphin county, from 1725 to 1790, we are inclined to think the following list comprises most, if not all, the heads of families of this congregation from 1745–55. All the names are on the tax list from

1750 to 1766; many for twenty years previously. After the Revolution they disappear year by year, and names of other nationalities take their places:

Alexander Bence,	Richard Grice,	Thomas M'Kee,
Thomas Bowman,	Hugh Hall, ·	Robert M'Kee,
John Bowman,	Widow Hall,	John M'Queen,
Abraham Bridgot,	John Hall,	Joseph M'Queen,
Thomas Breese,	Thomas Hall,	James M'Queen,
Hugh Black,	Jebel Hall,	Edward Queen,
Peter Corby,	James Hall,	Cornelius Queen,
James Crouch,	John Kerr,	James Rea,
James Clarke,	Thomas Kar,	John Rea, [or Wray,]
Hugh Clark,	Malcolm Karr,	William Rea,
Rowland Chambers,	Thomas Lenox,	Thomas Rutherford,
Arthur Chambers,	Tho. Mitchell,	William Shaw,
Robert Chambers,	Peter Murdoch,	Robert Spear,
Joseph Candor,	Robert Murdoch,	Adam Thomas,
Thomas Clark,	James Murdoch,	Tho. Wallace,
John Combe,	John Murdoch,	William White,
George Davidson,	Neil M'Allister,	Archibald Walker,
John Doakes,	John M'Allister,	James Walker,
Arch'd Elliott,	John M'Nair,	William Work.
George Gray,		

The foregoing list of names would show a population of about two hundred in 1740.

That part of Dauphin county we are writing of was originally the township of Derry, in Lancaster county, and "set off" at the first court in 1729. In 1768 a part of Derry was "set off" and called Londonderry, "commencing by a road leading from Conewago creek by the Widow *Hall's*, &c. In 1826 rectification of lines was ordered, when finally, in 1850, Conewago township was "set off" from the east end of Londonderry, leaving the site we have been endeavoring to describe, in Londonderry, a short mile north-east of Geinburg, three miles from Middletown, seven miles from Paxtang church, four miles from Derry Spring, and about six miles from Donegal, all noted Presbyterian settlements.

Another, a family burial-place, is about half a mile west of the one belonging to the Conewago congregation. The inscriptions on the stones scattered about are in German, and all bear the name of "Gein." This spot, as well as its neighbor, is in a disgraceful state of neglect.

The surroundings of the Conewago place of burial are charming and romantic. Almost under the shadow of the frowning "Round Top," on the north and west—the Cornwall Hills on the east—and in the more distant south the South mountain shows its broken front. The farms are kept in very handsome condition, a generous soil is carefully cultivated, the improvements and enclosures substantial, and at present inhabited almost entirely by persons of German descent. There are not half a dozen families of Scotch-Irish descent in the neighborhood.

Many admirers of the sturdy race who first formed congregations and conquered the virgin soil of this part of Pennsylvania think that the Presbytery of Carlisle should take order on the subject of vacant burial-grounds within its bounds. There are four such plots in Dauphin county, and soon a fifth will be added, if historic "Derry" is allowed to be pulled to pieces to satisfy the curiosity or vandalism of those who use its venerated soil for pic-nics and frolics not quite so reputable.

NOTES.

A perusal of these brief notes will awaken interest in many quarters touching early family records or tradition, and may be the means of establishing the correctness of the narrative, and perhaps of recovering papers whose contents will further elucidate the early history of the settlements along the Susquehanna "above Conewago"—a field of inquiry almost untrodden.

Mr. Black, the only pastor we have been enabled to name, was from Ulster; was licensed by the Newcastle Presbytery in 1735, when he was chosen pastor of the "Forks of Brandywine." In 1738 he presided at the installation of Rev. John Elder, at Paxtang. In October, 1741, he came to "Conewago." In 1743 he appears to have gone "missionary to South Mountain," in Virginia. He died there in 1770 "an aged minister."

Hugh Hall's wife was a daughter of James Roddy, who was on the first grand jury held in Lancaster county, and whose name appears on the assessment of Donegal in 1723. He was active in all the affairs of the Donegal settlement. Roddy resided some miles south of Conewago.

Hugh Hall had a son Hugh Hall, who was an ensign in Colonel (General) Hugh Mercer's "third battalion of sixteen companies, May 4, 1758." Opposite his name on the roll is written "of a reputable and good family in Lancaster county." Their captain was Adam Read, Esquire, the father-in-law of John Harris, by his second marriage, and the lieutenant was John Simpson, father of General Michael Simpson. All these officers were citizens of the territory of what thirty years after became Dauphin county.

The M'Queens so numerous in this congregation have mostly become M'Cunes. The orthography of the list of taxables about 1750 is something wonderful. Just as the assessor talked he wrote. If a man paid his tax he was marked "pate;" if Kerr was assessed, he was enrolled Carr, and so with all the rest, even to dropping the national "Mac" from the M'Queens, reducing the name to Queen; in some instances M'Guinne and M'Quown.

The Kerrs came to Conewago in 1730. One of the family became the Rev. William Kerr of Donegal, who married a granddaughter of the Rev. John Elder. Representatives of the family, in almost all its branches, still reside in Dauphin county—an instance of stability and content to be noted in the restless race from which it sprung.

Jane Murdoch, the daughter of John and sister of James, married Thomas Rutherford in 1732. The Murdochs then lived "above Conoy." This marriage has numerous descendants in Dauphin county, and in many of the western counties of this and other States.

The family of Work removed to the west early after the Revolution.

The Clarks are found in all parts of Pennsylvania and the west. A son of one of them was an officer of rank in the Revolution, and some of his descendants yet reside in this county.

A daughter of John M'Queen, Rosanna, married Capt. Jamieson of Donegal.

David M'Nair has descendants yet residing in Dauphin county. I think Hon. John M'Nair, formerly member of Congress from the Montgomery district, informed me that "his people originally settled on the Susquehanna."

Adam Thomas owned a farm just north of the grave-yard, and was uncle to the venerable Mrs. Valentine Egle, of Harrisburg, who died in Harrisburg, August 5, 1867, at the great age of ninety-five. Thomas was a Welshman.

This family of Chambers permanently established themselves below Harris ferry.

James Crouch became a prominent man in Revolutionary times. He was a colonel.

Hugh Black's family has no descendants in the male line.

Both M'Kees were Indian traders. James and his descendants remained on the land he warranted in 1737 until about 1830, when the family name is lost. The famous Belle of it was an only heir, married, and removed to a distant county. Thomas, about 1753, removed to his "upper farm, about thirty miles from Harris ferry," where he built a fort. He was an officer under Burd at Forts Augusta and Hunter, and his singular orthography figures in long pages of letters printed in the Pennsylvania Archives.

The Wallace family, possibly descendants of the one belonging to this congregation, settled in great force along the Swatara creek, in Derry and Hanover.

The family of Wray were numerous in Hanover at a later date.

Candor and Lenox are names not often found in Dauphin county at present. It is not known to what part of the country they emigrated. One of the name died at Harrisburg forty years ago.

FEBRUARY, 1877.

NEW-SIDE

PRESBYTERIAN GRAVE-YARD,

Lower Paxtang Township,

DAUPHIN COUNTY.

NEW-SIDE GRAVE-YARD.

THE "new side Presbyterians" were those followers of the Tennents, Blairs, Carmichael and others who agreed with them in antagonism to the Synod of Philadelphia. The Newcastle Presbytery being "new side" licensed Rev. John Roan in 1744. He came about 1747 to Derry, Mount Joy and Paxtang, gathering small congregations in each of these localities. It is not known that any other church was erected for him except the one at Mount Joy. His people did not use Paxtang grave-yard, selecting the one we are about to describe for their use.

Its situation is distant from the common routes of the present day, and indeed is known to very few. It is in Lower Paxtang township, Dauphin county, six miles east of Harrisburg, two miles north of Paxtang church, nine miles south-west of Hanover church, on the road from Harrisburg to Hornerstown and Union Deposit. There is no appearance of any structure ever having been erected upon it. Yet it will be seen that there is evidence that a small one was erected on or near the spot. In an advertisement of the day we find that on the eleventh of September, 1795, James Byers and James Willson, executors of William Brown, Esq., deceased, of Paxtang, offered for sale "a LOG-HOUSE near the residence formerly occupied as a house of worship by the Reverend Matthew Lind." This, and the thirty-four acres of land, appears to have been purchased by George Weidman; afterwards by George Shirk; then by Jacob Grove, whose family reside there at present—1877.

The "log-house," formerly occupied as "a house of worship," was used, within the memory of many persons yet living, as a sheep-pen. It stood north of the grave-yard, but close to it. It has disappeared.

The Rev. Mr. Lind was a member of Carlisle Presbytery, and is known to have often preached within its bounds. The enclosure contains less than one acre of ground, and is at present in tolerable repair. The earliest interment was made in 1750—the last about 1855, showing its use for more than one hundred years.

Many graves unmarked, show that interments have not been made for many years. It has not been used for at least twenty. The liberality and attention of Mr. Robert Stewart, of Hanover, has kept its enclosure in fair condition. Some organization of Presbyterians should take this burial-place in charge, and provide for repairs every few years. Any public-spirited citizen, no matter what his religious affiliations, would cheerfully contribute labor so supreme, and feel true happiness in doing so.

Directly after entering the enclosure we find plain slabs, some of red sand stone, others of more pretentious marble, others of wood, marked as follows:

In
Memory
of
William M'Clure
Who Departed
This Life April
1785
Aged 54 years

Here
Lyeth the Body
of John Stewart
of Dauphin county
Hanover Township
Who Departed
This Life the 8th
of April 1777
aged 63 years

Here
Lyeth the Body
of Agnes Stewart
Late Spouse of
Hugh Stewart of
Paxton who Depar
ted this Life the
22d of March 1790
aged 55 years

Here Lyeth the
body of
Hugh Stewart of
Paxton who departed
this Life the 8th of Oct
1798 Aged 80 years
Also
Hannah Stewart
Spouse of said Stewart
who departed this
Life the 8th Oct. 1750 Aged
33 years

In
Memory of
Sarah
wife of
Robert Stewart
Born Aug 10, 1768
Died May 8, 1813
Aged 44 yrs, 8 mo's
& 29 days

In
Memory of
Robert Stewart
Born March 8, 1765
Died April 4, 1854
Aged 89 years & 26 d.

G.   1766   M.
Here Layeth
The Body of
Margery
Marshal
Died Jan'y ye 6, 1766
Aged 21 Years
& 5 months

In Memory of
Mary Welch
Who Dec'd August
22nd 1754 Aged 47
Years
Also Jean Welch
Who Dec'd Sept.
3th 1754 aged 18
Years

In Memory of
James Welch w
ho Deceased Ja
nuary ye 28d 1754
aged 50 years
Also James Welch
Younger who Dec'd
August 7th 1754 Aged
20 years

In
Memory
of
William Duncan
Who Departed
This Life Sept 24
1783
Aged 97 Years

In
Memory
of
James Duncan
Who Departed
This Life Aug't 25th
1792
Aged 68 years.

In
Memory of
Joseph Willson
Sen'r Who Departed
this Life the 7 day Feb'y
1799 aged 84 Years
Also
Jean his First Wife
Departed this Life the
11th of April 1763 Aged
43 Years

In the quiet grave-yard at Brown's Mill, six miles south of Chambersburg, Franklin county, Pennsylvania, rest the remains of, perchance, the only pastor of the "New-Side Congregation." On two plain marble slabs, side by side, are the following inscriptions:

Sacred | to | the Memory | of | the Rev. Matthew Lind | Who after having served God in the | Gospel of his Son for nearly forty years | and performed with exemplary tenderness | and fidelity the duties resulting from | his relations in life fell asleep in Jesus | on the 21st of April 1800 aged 68 years | and 8 months | Blessed are the dead who die in the Lord.

———

In | Memory | of | Jennie Fulton | Consort | of | the Rev. Matthew Lind | Among wives the most dutiful; among | mothers the most affectionate, and among | friends the kindest and most hospitable, | her name will be always dear to those who | knew her. She died on the first day of | April 1819, in the seventy-third year of | her age | Precious in the sight of the Lord | is the death of his Saints.

www.ingramcontent.com/pod-product-compliance
Lightning Source LLC
Chambersburg PA
CBHW060809110426
42739CB00032BA/3156